Woah /
Kent, Deborah.

4755

J 97 KEN

LANCASTER VETERANS MEMORIAL LIBRARY

3 8420 0060 28

W9-BFG-074

Utah

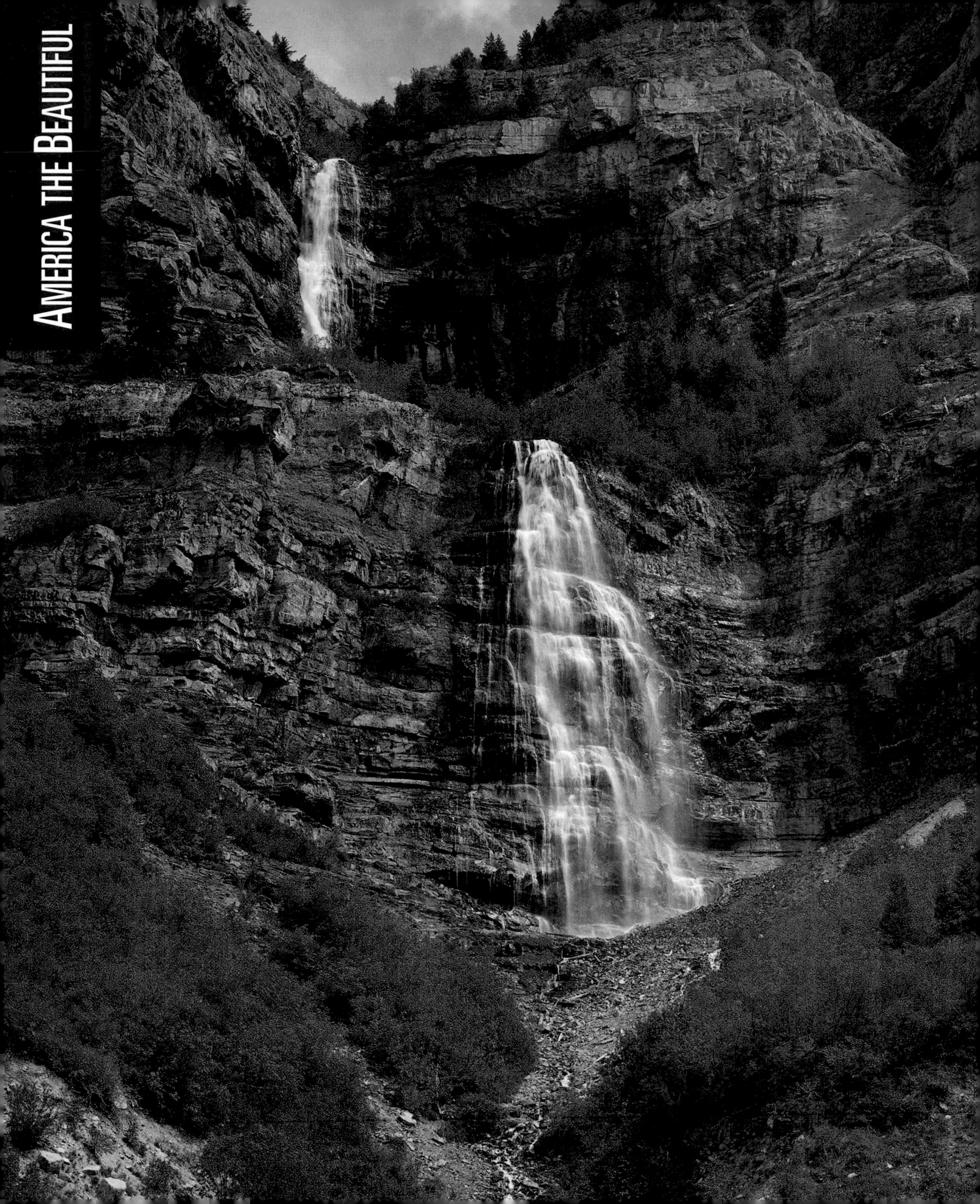

Utah

Deborah Kent

Children's Press®
A Division of Grolier Publishing
New York   London   Hong Kong   Sydney
Danbury, Connecticut

LANCASTER VETERANS MEMORIAL LIBRARY
LANCASTER, TX.

Frontispiece: Bridal Veil Falls, Provo River canyon

Front cover: Salt Lake City

Back cover: Glen Canyon National Park Recreation Area

Consultant: Marilyn Getts, Branch Manager, Central Branch Library,
Davis County Library System

Please note: All statistics are as up-to-date as possible at the time of publication.

Visit Children's Press on the Internet at http://publishing.grolier.com

Book production by Editorial Directions, Inc.

Library of Congress Cataloging-in-Publication Data

Kent, Deborah.
   Utah / by Deborah Kent.
      144 p. 24 cm. — (America the beautiful. Second series)
   Includes bibliographical references and index.
   Summary: An introduction to the geography, natural resources, history, economy,
     important sites, daily life, and people of Utah.
   ISBN 0-516-21045-9
   1. Utah—Juvenile literature. [1. Utah.] I. Title. II. Series.
F826.3.K46 2000
979.2—dc21   99-11689
                                                     CIP
                                                      AC

©2000 by Children's Press®, a division of Grolier Publishing Co., Inc.
All rights reserved. Published simultaneously in Canada
Printed in the United States of America
1 2 3 4 5 6 7 8 9 10 R 09 08 07 06 05 04 03 02 01 00

Acknowledgments

I wish to thank the Utah Historical Society, the Utah Department of Tourism, and the Salt Lake City Chamber of Commerce. Their staffs went far beyond the call of duty to help me gather information and ideas for the preparation of this book.

Behind-the-Rocks

Pinnacle and the Canyonlands

Wasatch Mountain Range

Contents

A dipper

Mountain biking

Salt Lake City

Skiing at Alta

Anasazi pottery

CHAPTER ONE

Glory in the Desert

The Mormon Tabernacle is known for its oval dome.

Every year during the Christmas season, Temple Square in Salt Lake City, Utah, sparkles with lights. Strings of gleaming bulbs outline every bush and tree. Lights play along the benches and dance over the fountains and rocks. Against the evening sky, Temple Square is illuminated, brilliant and alive.

The Christmas display in Temple Square is immensely popular with native Utahns and visitors alike. People flock to the square by the thousands. Standing in the crowd, you know you are at the heart of a remarkable city.

Temple Square is the geographic and spiritual hub of Salt Lake City, the capital of the state of Utah. Enclosed by a 15-foot (4.6-meter) stone wall, the square sprawls over 10 acres (4 hectares) of land. Paths wander beneath shade trees and zigzag through neatly tended gardens. Statues and monuments celebrate important moments in the history of the state.

Opposite: A snowy evening at Temple Square

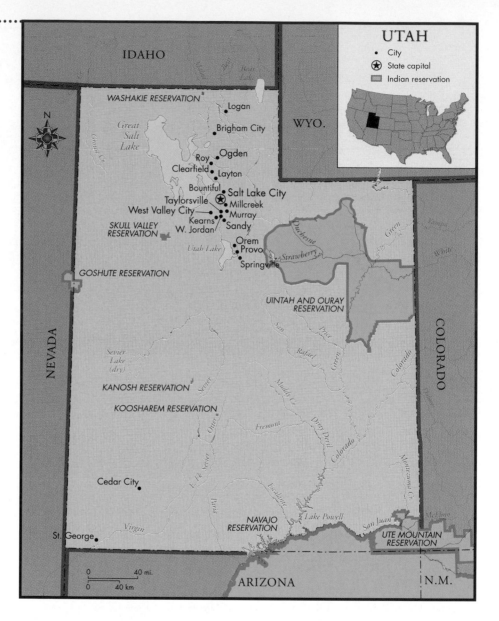

Geographical map of Utah

Presiding over the square is the temple of the Church of Jesus Christ of Latter-day Saints. The Latter-day Saints, as they are officially known, are usually referred to as Mormons. The temple on the square is a splendid granite structure crowned by six spires. Opposite the temple stands the famous Mormon Tabernacle with its unique oval dome. These two buildings are among Utah's most cherished landmarks. They are testaments to the faith and industry of the Mormons, the first people of European descent to settle Utah's Great Salt Lake valley.

The story of Utah is closely bound to the story of the Mormons. Members of this religious group reached present-day Utah in 1847, determined to establish the Holy Kingdom of Zion on Earth. Mormon influence remains strong in Utah today. But people from many other backgrounds also make Utah their home and help to shape the state's culture and economy. Native American traditions are kept alive by people of Ute, Paiute, and Shoshone descent. Persons of Mexican heritage have a major impact in many parts of the state. And everywhere Utah carries reminders that Roman Catholics, Jews, and members of every Protestant denomination have a role in the state's development. Despite the powerful Mormon presence, ethnic and religious diversity is very much part of life in Utah. Utah is a crossroads of the West, a place where diverse peoples meet, work, and live together.

When the Mormon pioneers reached Utah, they saw a land of rugged mountains and sun-baked deserts. In many places, water was scarce and trees were few. To their amazement, the newcomers discovered an immense lake with salty water, similar to the ocean. Utah was a pitiless land that tested every man, woman, and child. But it was also a land rich with possibilities. The pioneers worked tirelessly to create gardens in the desert and thriving towns in the valleys.

Today Utahns no longer see the land as an adversary, but as a precious resource. Beneath the deserts and mountains lie vast

deposits of coal, oil, and natural gas. In addition, Utah's scenic landscape lures visitors from around the world. In winter, skiers swoop down the steep mountain slopes. Summer brings hikers and mountain climbers. Millions of people pour into the state to explore the national parks at Zion, Canyonlands, and Arches.

Utahns have shaped the land in which they live, but the land has also shaped them. It has made them strong and resourceful and graced them with a love of the outdoors. To understand the character of the state and its people, let's look back at Utah's fascinating history.

Opposite: Utah's breathtaking scenery draws visitors from around the world.

CHAPTER TWO

An Unimagined Country

A variety of animals inhabited the canyons of what is now Utah.

"The Indian people have roots here in this country. When people bother the remains of the ancients, it is us they are bothering. Those who tell others to leave the dwellings and rock markings alone are speaking for the Indians. They are landmarks in sacred areas. They remind the world that the people once lived there."

—Clifford Duncan, a Ute Indian from Utah's Uintah Basin

The First to Venture

Sometime around 11,000 B.C., a band of hunters ventured into the land we now know as Utah. They were the descendants of nomadic peoples who probably crossed the Bering Strait from Siberia into North America. In the forests and mountains of Utah, the hunters discovered bison, elk, deer, and other animals that still live there. They also found woolly mammoths, saber-toothed tigers, and

Opposite: Anasazi ruins at Cedars State Historical Monument

American camels—species that have long since disappeared. Year after year, more people came to Utah to hunt. They explored its mountains and canyons and made the region their home.

Traces of Utah's earliest residents have been found in the natural caves where they lived. These people chipped stone spear points and axes, and they made awls, scrapers, and other tools out of bone. Hunting spears were hurled with a notched stick called an atlatl. The added thrust of the atlatl sent the spear flying with tremendous force.

Some time about 2,000 years ago, people in Utah learned to grow corn. The cultivation of corn changed the lives of Utah's wandering hunters. People began to settle in villages so that they could tend their crops. Their houses consisted of pits in the ground that were lined with flat stones. These pit houses were roofed over with poles plastered with mud. At about the same time, the early Utahns began weaving sturdy baskets from the fibers of the yucca and other plants. Some of these baskets were woven so tightly that they could hold water without leaking a drop. The Basketmakers, as they are called, lived in southern Utah, northern New Mexico, and parts of Arizona and Colorado. After several hundred years, the land was taken over by a people known to us as the Anasazi. The name *Anasazi* comes from a Navajo word meaning "old ones." The Anasazi may be the ancestors of the Pueblo peoples who now live in New Mexico.

In about A.D. 900, the Anasazi began to build multistoried dwellings on the cliffs of New Mexico, Arizona, and southern Utah. Like apartment houses, these cliff dwellings provided homes for many families. Their houses climbed the cliffs in a series of ter-

The Anasazi built cliff dwellings.

An example of Anasazi pottery

races, the roof of one serving as the porch or balcony of the home above. A wooden ladder provided an entrance to each apartment. When the ladders were pulled inside, the cliff dwellers were protected from enemy attack.

The Anasazi raised corn, beans, and squash in fields near their homes. They raised turkeys and made clothing from strips of turkey skin. The Anasazi were also master potters. They shaped clay into jugs and bowls, baking them in a pit to give them extra strength.

Written in Stone

Here and there across Utah, ancient pictures gaze from the smooth stone cliffs. Some of these pictures were carved into the stone with sharp tools. Others are paintings, now fading but still recognizable. The carved pictures are called petroglyphs, and the paintings are known as pictographs.

Most of these ancient stone pictures show human figures or animals such as bison, deer, and mountain lions. Some rock art depicts scenes of hunting or warfare.

Petroglyphs and pictographs were not a form of written language, and people have differing ideas about their significance. Many researchers think they may have played a role in certain religious ceremonies. Others feel that they may be family histories or that they provided information for travelers. Perhaps some were created by artists who drew them for pleasure. ■

The Anasazi stored grain in protected bins such as these.

This advanced Anasazi culture flourished until the middle of the 1300s. Then the Anasazi suddenly abandoned their villages, scattering to the south and west. Perhaps a prolonged drought caused their crops to fail. Or perhaps they were attacked by nomadic tribes from the north. Whatever the reason, the Anasazi never returned to their cliff dwellings.

When Europeans reached present-day Utah, they found three groups of Native American people living in the region. The Ute, for whom Utah is named, lived in the eastern half of the state. Western Utah was home to the Paiute and the Shoshone. A subgroup of the Shoshone was called the Goshute. The Ute, Paiute, and Shoshone were divided into many small bands, each with its own chief. The eight Ute bands included the Timpanogo, Yampa, and Uinta. The bands had no central government, though they shared languages and customs.

The Indians of Utah lived mainly by hunting animals and gathering wild fruits, roots, and berries. Sometimes a band worked together to chase bison over a cliff or to herd jackrabbits into an enclosure made of sticks and underbrush. Some Paiute in the harsh deserts of southwestern Utah developed a taste for ants and grasshoppers. When other food was scarce, these insects were a plentiful source of protein.

Life for Utah's native peoples flowed through the seasons with hunger and feasting, warfare and peace. But events in a land far to the south would change this way of life forever.

Native Americans hunted antelope and other game on the Utah plains.

Friars from the South

To most Americans, the date 1776 brings only one event to mind—the signing of the Declaration of Independence by delegates from the thirteen British colonies. But far to the west, the year 1776 marked a major event in the history of Utah. On July 29, just twenty-five days after the Declaration of Independence was signed in Philadelphia, a small Spanish expedition set out from Santa Fe, New Mexico. The expedition was led by two priests, Father Silvestre Velez de Escalante and Father Francisco Atanasio Dominguez. Escalante and Dominguez hoped to find an overland route from Santa Fe to California.

In 1776, Spain controlled much of the Western Hemisphere. The region known as New Spain sprawled from Central America in the south to Santa Fe in the north. Spain had also established a chain of missions on the California coast. At the missions, priests converted Indians to Roman Catholicism and put them to work on farms or ranches. At that time, California could be reached only by

Troubled Sleep

"The first grave I ever dug was when I was three years old," Earl K. Shumway admitted in 1986. "Around here it's not a crime, it's a way of life." Shumway was referring to grave robbing, the practice of digging up Anasazi graves to rob them of the pottery, weapons, and other objects buried with the dead. Sold on the black market to private collectors, such artifacts can fetch up to $50,000.

Native American graves are protected by federal law, and grave robbers can be fined and sent to prison. But, for many decades, grave robbing was common in Utah because not enough government agents patrolled the vast tracts of land where the grave sites are found.

In the early 1990s, officials increased their efforts to protect Indian graves. In 1994, Shumway, one of Utah's most notorious grave robbers, was sentenced to a prison term of 6 1/2 years. Burial sites are a sacred part of Native American heritage, and the crackdown on grave robbers helps ensure that the sites are treated with respect. ■

sea. Officials in Mexico City, the capital of New Spain, hoped to bind California more closely to their empire by finding a route across the mountains and deserts.

Escalante and Dominguez entered Utah from the east and traveled along the White River. Eventually they crossed the Green River and camped with a band of Ute on Utah Lake. The Ute described a mysterious body of water somewhere to the north. "The other lake . . . covers many leagues, so we were informed, and its waters are harmful and extremely salty," Escalante wrote in his journal. "The [Timpanogo] assured us that anyone who wet some part of the body with [the waters] immediately felt a lot of itching in the part moistened."

The priests did not investigate this strange story. They were looking for navigable mountain passes and rivers that were easy to cross. Instead they found unscalable peaks and rivers lost

Father Escalante in the Utah Valley

between steep canyon walls. After months of struggle, many in the party wanted to turn back. The expedition leaders decided to place the matter in God's hands. "Concluding our prayers, we cast lots, and it came out in favor of [returning to New Mexico]," Escalante wrote. "We all accepted this, thanks be to God, willingly and joyfully."

The travelers returned to Santa Fe in January 1777. They had been the first people of European ancestry to explore the region that is now Utah. The expedition's cartographer, Bernardo Miera y Pacheco, made detailed maps of the land he had seen. His maps also included features he had heard of from the Indians but had not actually seen. He showed the great lake with the salty water. He also indicated a river he called the Buenaventura. According to Miera y Pacheco's maps, the Buenaventura flowed all the way to the Pacific Ocean.

Escalante and Dominguez reported that there was no practical route to California across the wasteland to the north. New Spain's officials did not question their word. They had far greater concerns. Spain was weakening, and its power in the Americas was beginning to crumble. There were no resources to spare for exploring the barren Utah country.

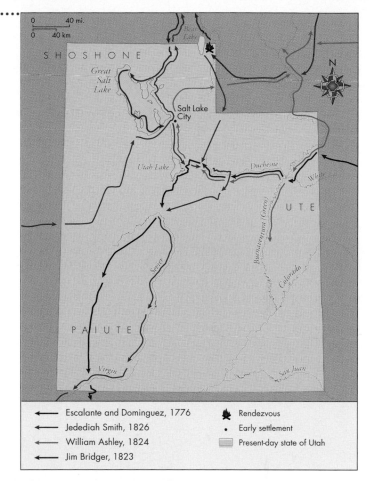

0   40 mi.
0   40 km

SHOSHONE
Great Salt Lake
Salt Lake City
Utah Lake
Duchesne
White
Buenaventura (Green)
UTE
Sevier
Colorado
PAIUTE
Virgin
San Juan

← Escalante and Dominguez, 1776
← Jedediah Smith, 1826
← William Ashley, 1824
← Jim Bridger, 1823
🔥 Rendezvous
• Early settlement
▭ Present-day state of Utah

Exploration map of Utah

Yet, over the years that followed, a few bold Spanish traders pushed north along the route Escalante had followed. They made regular visits to the Ute at Utah Lake, trading Spanish blankets and kettles for furs. Contact with the Europeans introduced the Indians to horses, alcohol, and guns. Some Ute and Shoshone became expert riders.

The Ute had frequent contact with the European settlers.

On the Trail of the Beaver

After Escalante's expedition, the Spaniards considered Utah part of their territory, but they made no effort to settle the region. When Americans from the East began to explore Utah early in the 1800s, Spain could do nothing to stop them. During this period, no well-dressed gentleman in London or Paris could step outside without wearing a beaver hat, and every fashionable lady wore a beaver cape and carried a beaver muff. Because most of these rich furs came from North America, beavers had almost disappeared from the Atlantic Coast area. But in the unsettled West the supply seemed inexhaustible.

John Jacob Astor sent expeditions of fur trappers into the Utah wilderness.

John Jacob Astor, an American merchant, made his fortune by trading in beaver, otter, and other furs. From his headquarters in Oregon Country, Astor sent trapping expeditions into the wild country to the east. In 1811, one such expedition reached the mountains of western Utah. Astor's men traded with the Indians, exchanging guns and rum for furs. Soon other fur-trading companies sent trappers and traders to Utah.

The fur traders of early Utah were a breed apart. Often referred to as mountain men, they shunned life in towns and cities. Traveling alone for weeks or months at a time, they learned to survive in the wilderness by hunting, fishing, and gathering nuts and fruits. They mastered Ute, Shoshone, and other Indian languages,

LANCASTER VETERANS MEMORIAL LIBRARY
LANCASTER, TX.

Fur trading on the Bear River

The Fall of New Spain

For 300 years, Spain controlled Mexico and a huge area of land to the north. Its claims spread from Texas to California and extended into Colorado and Utah. However, Spain lacked the resources to colonize its northern territories, and its hold on them was never strong. In 1821, Mexico broke away from Spain to become an independent republic. The northern reaches of New Spain, including Spanish Utah, became part of this new nation. But Mexico, like Spain, made no attempt to establish settlements in Utah. The territory was Mexican in name only. ■

and they adopted many Native American customs. A number of the mountain men became legends in their own time and are still remembered by lovers of Western lore.

In 1824, mountain man Jim Bridger was working for a trader named William H. Ashley. On an expedition into northwestern Utah, Bridger and his party came upon Utah's most striking natural phenomenon, the Great Salt Lake. Many historians consider Bridger to be the first person of European descent to see the lake. Its waters stretched toward the horizon like a vast inland sea. At first, Bridger thought he had found an arm of the Pacific Ocean, but in 1826, four men circled the lake and found that it was entirely self-contained.

The Bible and the Gun

In general, the mountain men were a rough, hard-drinking lot. But Jedediah Smith (1799–1831) shunned alcohol. It was said that he traveled with a gun in one hand and a Bible in the other. Smith was a fearless fighter and explorer. In 1826, he set out from Great Salt Lake with a party of traders, crossed the deserts of present-day Nevada, and reached the California coast. Smith made two more hard journeys between Utah and California. At the age of thirty-two, he was killed in a skirmish with Indians on the Santa Fe Trail. ■

William H. Ashley, another mountain man, finally dispelled the myth that a river led from Utah to the Pacific Ocean. Ashley was determined to find the Buenaventura River that Miera y Pacheco had shown on his maps. In a boat made of bison hide, Ashley set off down the Green River but found only rock-strewn canyons and impassable rapids. Later he wrote, "The river is bounded by

The Man of Many Tongues

Jim Bridger, a mountain man, was also a brilliant linguist. He spoke French, Spanish, and a dozen Indian languages. He also had an uncanny ability to collect information on the trail—from footprints, hoof marks, and the ashes of fires. With his mastery of Indian languages, Bridger traveled freely among the Native Americans of the western frontier.

Bridger joined his first fur-trading expedition at the age of eighteen. For the next twenty years, he traded with the Indians across a vast area that included Utah. During the 1850s, Bridger became a scout for the U.S. Army. In 1861, he led the Berthoud Expedition that discovered a route through the mountains west of Denver, Colorado. The Berthoud Pass became a vital link between Denver and Salt Lake City, Utah. ■

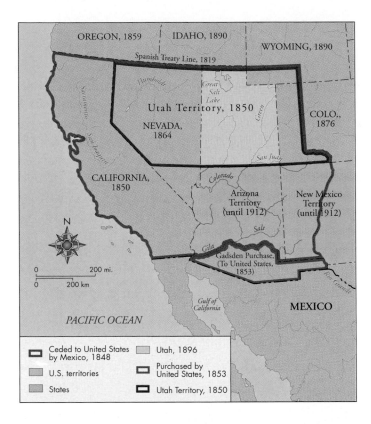

Historical map of Utah

Getting Together

Once a year the mountain men came down from the hills to trade their furs at the annual "rendezvous." The rendezvous was the major social event in the region. It was a time for trading stories as well as furs, a time for drinking, singing, gambling, and sometimes getting into fights. Visitors can experience a somewhat tamer version of the rendezvous at Fort Buenaventura near Ogden. Campfires flicker, and old songs are sung again. Men and women in tepees demonstrate traditional crafts such as making moccasins from soft leather.

Fort Buenaventura was founded as a military outpost and trading center by mountain man Miles Goodyear. Today's fort is a replica of Goodyear's original. ◼

lofty mountains heaped together in the greatest disorder, exhibiting a surface as barren as can be imagined."

But the mountain men did find a usable trail through the Rocky Mountains—a passage known as South Pass. For more than thirty years, pack mules loaded with bundles of pelts made their way through South Pass, then south to Santa Fe. From there, the furs traveled along the famous Santa Fe Trail to Missouri for shipment to ports in the East.

When Jim Bridger first saw the Great Salt Lake, he thought it connected to the Pacific Ocean.

Historians estimate that only about 100 mountain men ever lived in Utah at any given time, but they helped to establish an American presence in the region. In 1846, the United States launched a war against Mexico. The war ended in 1848 with a treaty that gave an immense tract of territory to the United States. Mexico lost Arizona, New Mexico, and Texas, and gave up all claims to its remote northern territories. The area called Utah then belonged to the United States.

CHAPTER THREE

Building the Kingdom

"We cannot purchase wagons and teams as in years past. I am consequently thrown back on my old plan, and that is to make handcarts and let the immigrants foot it. They can come just as quick, if not quicker, and much cheaper; can start earlier and escape the prevailing sickness which annually lays so many of our brethren in the dust."

—Brigham Young, president of the Church of Jesus Christ of Latter-day Saints, 1856

The angel Moroni delivering the two gold plates to Joseph Smith

Visions and Dreams

While the mountain men explored Utah's rivers and canyons, a fourteen-year-old boy named Joseph Smith (1805–1844) struggled with a spiritual crisis in western New York. Smith was confused by the variety of Protestant churches in his community. In his prayers, he asked God to show him which faith he ought to follow. Later, Smith said that God and Jesus appeared to him and told him to found the true religion. The nature of this religion was eventually revealed to him through a series of visions. In one, Smith claimed, an angel named Moroni gave him two gold plates. The plates, or tablets, were inscribed with a sacred message. With the help of "two stones in silver bows . . . fastened to a breastplate," Smith translated the text into English. Moroni then took back the plates, and Smith began his mission.

Opposite: Brigham Young at the Great Salt Lake

Joseph Smith preaching to his followers

In 1830, Joseph Smith published the Book of Mormon, his translation of Moroni's message. He described it as a new book of the Bible, to follow the Old and New Testaments. According to the Book of Mormon, Jesus Christ appeared several times in North and South America. The book prophesied that Christ will come again, and it called on the people to make ready.

Soon after publishing the Book of Mormon, Smith founded the Church of Jesus Christ of Latter-day Saints (sometimes called the LDS Church) at Fayette, New York. The Latter-day Saints are widely referred to as the Mormons, after the Book of Mormon that is central to their faith. With Smith as its first president, the church won converts by the hundreds, and then by the thousands. Smith and his followers moved to Kirtland, Ohio, and they later headed west to Independence, Missouri. Finally some 20,000 Mormons settled in Nauvoo, Illinois.

The Mormons were hardworking people who prospered wherever they went. But non-Mormons (known to the Mormons as Gentiles) regarded them with suspicion. The Mormons were too numerous and too powerful. Some Mormon beliefs seemed strange and frightening to traditional Christians. Then, in 1843, rumors of a new doctrine spread throughout the Mormon community. People began to hear that Smith allowed Mormon men to practice polygamy—to have more than one wife at the same time. The practice of polygamy outraged non-Mormons and even caused a split within the LDS Church. In 1844, Joseph Smith and his brother Hyrum were imprisoned in the Illinois town of Carthage. Before they could stand trial, a mob broke into the jail, and both men were murdered.

After the death of Joseph Smith, the presidency of the Mormon Church passed to a former carpenter named Brigham Young. Young decided to lead the Mormons to a place where they would be safe from persecution. Countless American families were streaming westward along the Oregon Trail, hoping to find a better life on the Pacific Coast. But Young did not want to join this throng. He wanted to find a place where there were no other settlers, where the Mormons could establish their "abiding place," sometimes referred to as "the Kingdom of Zion." "If there is a place on earth that nobody else wants," Young declared, "that's the place I am hunting for."

In 1844, a mob stormed the jail in which Joseph Smith was being held and murdered him.

In 1846, Young led the Mormons from Illinois to Winter Quarters—near Omaha, Nebraska—where they spent a long, hard winter. Many died of hunger and disease. As soon as the weather was warm enough for travel, Young gathered an advance party of 143 men, 3 women, and 2 children. With these faithful followers, he struck out across the Great Plains and into the Rocky Mountains. At first, he followed old maps drawn by early explorers. Later, he met mountain man Jim Bridger, who helped the party on its way. Young's destination was the Salt Lake Valley of present-day Utah.

The Mormons endured bad weather and hunger as they crossed the plains.

On July 24, 1847, Brigham Young reached the mouth of Emigration Canyon and looked down upon the Salt Lake Valley for the first time. He was sick with a fever, but in the parched landscape he saw a glorious future. Here his followers could build a splendid city with broad streets and a holy temple. They could turn the desert into a garden. Gazing into the valley, Young exclaimed, "This is the place!"

Deseret

The Mormons took no time to relax after their long journey from Nebraska. As soon as they arrived in the Salt Lake Valley, they set to work. Even before they built houses to live in, they prepared the earth for planting. They dug ditches from City Creek to water the dry land. When the earth was moist and soft

A caravan of Mormons
on their way to Utah

enough, they broke it with plows. They knew that they had to plant crops as soon as possible to ensure a fall harvest and food for the winter.

For living quarters, the Mormons built a fort of sun-dried adobe brick. "Conditions within the fort were especially bad when it rained," wrote the pioneer Charles Coulson Rich. "For, the roofs having been made with too little slant, small streams of thin mud trickled down upon those underneath, and it so happened that, on such occasions, the only protection was the hoisted umbrella. . . . And there were the bugs and mice." Conditions were miserable, but the pioneers met them bravely. They knew they must prepare a home for the migrants who would follow them. Beyond that, they felt that their hard work was preparing them for life in the next world.

··

First Encampment

In 1997, to honor the 150th anniversary of the city's founding, First Encampment Park was established in Salt Lake City. The park marks the location where the Mormon pioneers camped until they could build permanent shelters. The names of the members of Brigham Young's first pioneer band are carved into boulders in the park. ■

The Apostles—the highest Mormon leaders—wanted to grace their homeland with a splendid city, and they gave it on a grand design. Each city block would cover 10 acres (4 ha). The main streets would be 132 feet (40 m) wide, flanked by broad, tree-lined sidewalks. At the heart of the city would stand the magnificent Mormon Temple, the crown jewel of the new land. The city became Salt Lake City, named in honor of the Great Salt Lake nearby. The Mormons called their territory the State of Deseret. The word "deseret," which came from the Book of Mormon, means "honeybee." To the Mormons, the honeybee was a symbol of industry and community.

By fall, Brigham Young was satisfied with progress in the Salt Lake Valley. Recovered from his illness, he returned to Nebraska, where the rest of the migrants waited patiently. It was no small matter to ready some 20,000 people for a journey by wagon across the

Quarrying stone for the Mormon Temple

The Leader of a People

Brigham Young (1801–1877) had been trained as a carpenter and furniture maker. He was working in western New York State when he read the Book of Mormon and heard the preachings of Joseph Smith. In 1832, Young was baptized in the Mormon Church. He rose quickly in the church leadership and took control when Smith was killed in 1844.

In 1847, Young led the first band of Mormon migrants to the Salt Lake Valley in Utah. The following year, he accompanied the main body of Mormons on their westward journey from Nebraska. Under Young's direction, Mormon settlement spread throughout Utah and into the present-day states of New Mexico, Arizona, Wyoming, Nevada, and California.

Brigham Young had twenty-seven wives and dozens of children. Interviewing him in 1859, Horace Greeley of the *New York Herald* wrote, "In appearance he is a portly, frank, good-natured, rather thickset man of fifty-five, seeming to enjoy life and to be in no particular hurry to get to heaven." ■

windswept plains and over the mountains. But Young was a master at inspiring and organizing his followers. He purchased supplies and arranged for guides to lead the expedition. At last, in the spring of 1848, the main body of Mormons was on the move.

The Mormons reached the Salt Lake Valley in a series of waves. After Young's main company from Nebraska came smaller groups—from New England, Mississippi, and even from England and Scandinavia. During the 1850s, thousands of Mormons hauled their possessions across the plains on handcarts. Many arrived sick and hungry, exhausted from the hardships of the trail. The newcomers always received a generous welcome from those who were there ahead of them. On one occasion, Young cut short a

Thousands of Mormons survived difficult journeys to reach Utah.

church service when a band of weary travelers stumbled into town. "Prayer is good," he said, "but when baked potatoes and pudding and milk are needed, prayer will not supply their place."

Despite the hardships, the Mormons went on with the work at hand. By 1849, Brigham Young's great city had taken shape. Engi-

The Miracle of the Gulls

In the spring of 1848, the Mormon colony faced a desperate food shortage. Many crops were destroyed by an unexpected June frost. Then swarms of crickets invaded the fields. It looked as though the insects would devour every sprig of wheat and every stalk of corn. But before they could do serious damage, a huge flock of gulls darkened the sky. The gulls settled onto the fields and gobbled up the crickets. After three days, the birds flew away as suddenly as they had come.

To the Mormons, the arrival of the gulls was a miracle. It proved that God was with them, protecting them from harm. The event is commemorated with the Seagull Monument (left), erected on Salt Lake City's Temple Square in 1913. The statue of three gulls was created by sculptor Mahonri Young, Brigham Young's grandson. ■

neer Howard Stansbury described it when he arrived in Deseret to survey Great Salt Lake. "A city has been laid out upon a magnificent scale, being nearly four miles in length and three in breadth," Stansbury wrote. "Through the city itself flows an unfailing stream of pure, sweet water, which by an ingenious mode of irrigation, is made to traverse each side of every street spreading life, verdure and beauty over what was heretofore a barren waste."

Above all, the Mormons believed in working together. Because they had been persecuted in the past, they felt they must stand strong and united in their new land. Property was owned by the group rather than by individuals. Food was distributed so that everyone had an equal share.

Engineer Howard Stansbury was sent to survey Great Salt Lake.

As soon as the Mormons were well established in the Salt Lake Valley, Brigham Young began to expand the colony. He sent groups to start communities up and down the Wasatch Range. Mormon settlement spread into present-day Wyoming, Colorado, New Mexico, Arizona, Nevada, and California. The Mormons were highly successfuls farmers, and their settlements flourished. But their startling success did not automatically win them friends and support.

The Struggle for Statehood

In 1850, the State of Deseret petitioned the U.S. Congress for admission to the Union. Congress denied the request for statehood and even rejected the name Deseret. It renamed the region Utah, after the Ute. Congress granted Utah the official status of U.S. territory, with its capital at Fillmore. The territorial boundaries

President James Buchanan

embraced both Utah and present-day Nevada. The territory was divided when Nevada became a state in 1864.

When Utah became a territory, the United States was being torn apart by the issue of slavery. Tensions were mounting between the slaveholding South and the antislavery North. Some Americans felt that polygamy was just as evil as slavery. A delegate to the 1856 Republican National Convention declared that slavery and polygamy were "the twin relics of barbarism." Ignoring such pointed disapproval, Mormon men went on with their "plural marriages."

To make matters worse, Utah Mormons paid little heed to the territorial officials sent from Washington. They regarded church law as superior to civil law, which was made by mere mortals. In 1857, U.S. president James Buchanan heard reports that Utah was in rebellion. Buchanan ordered U.S. Army forces to put down the

Clash of Cultures

With the onslaught of Mormon settlers, the Indians lost their hunting grounds in Utah Territory. Brigham Young tried to keep peace. He encouraged the settlers to treat the Indians kindly and to offer them food when they met. In part because of Young's policy of "feeding rather than fighting," relations between settlers and Indians in Utah were free from conflict for many years.

In 1853, a Ute chief named Wakara (1808?–1855) attacked several Mormon outposts. The conflict is known as the Walker War, from Wakara's English nickname—Walker. Hostilities between Indians and whites flared again with one of the worst massacres of Indians in the Far West. The Bear River Massacre took place on January 29, 1863, just north of the border between Utah and Idaho. In this battle, 200 volunteers from California, led by Colonel Patrick Edward Connor, attacked a northwestern Shoshone village and killed 250 of its residents, including 90 women and children. Later came the Black Hawk War of 1865. In 1867, most of the Ute were forced onto a reservation in the Uintah Basin. Skirmishes between Indians and settlers continued until 1872, when the Shoshone were driven from Utah to a reservation in Idaho. ■

uprising. Buchanan's decision launched an interlude known as the Utah War.

At once the Mormons prepared to defend themselves. They vowed they would burn Salt Lake City before they would let it fall into enemy hands. A Mormon company under Lot Smith carried out a series of lightning raids on U.S. Army supply wagons. Smith and his scouts destroyed tons of food and weapons without shedding a drop of blood. The destruction of their supplies forced the army to winter at Fort Bridger in Wyoming, 300 miles (483 km) from the Salt Lake Valley.

Troops sent by President Buchanan in a misguided attempt to control the Mormons

Within months, opinion back east turned against the Utah War. Lamenting the waste of federal money, newspapers nicknamed the conflict "Buchanan's Blunder." Buchanan sent Colonel Thomas L. Kane to Utah to negotiate terms of peace and, in the winter of 1858, Brigham Young accepted a compromise. Alfred Cumming became the official, federally appointed governor. But unofficially Young remained in control of Utah until his death nineteen years later. The U.S. Army troops marched to Camp Floyd, west of Utah Lake. The soldiers remained there for the next three years, until the outbreak of war between the Union and the Southern states.

The soldiers brought big changes to Mormon Utah. For the first time, there were saloons in Salt Lake City. Like mountain men at

Bloodshed at Mountain Meadow

The Utah War was almost free from bloodshed, save for one tragic incident. On September 11, 1857, a group of Mormons and their Paiute allies attacked a civilian wagon train as it crossed Utah Territory. The travelers, who came from Arkansas and Missouri, were on their way to California. The Mormons believed that the migrants were in league with the U.S. Army, and rumor had it that some members of the party had been involved in Joseph Smith's murder thirteen years before. The Mormons persuaded the travelers to surrender, assuring them they would not be harmed. But when the travelers laid down their weapons, the Mormons and Indians attacked them. Most of the 140 unarmed travelers were killed. This grievous episode is known as the Mountain Meadow Massacre. ■

a rendezvous of old, the soldiers drank, gambled, and got into fights. Mormon leaders bemoaned their sinful ways. But the soldiers were a ready market for corn, beef, and other farm produce, and prices soared.

During the 1860s, Utahns lost their sense of isolation. From 1860 to 1861, Pony Express riders galloped across the territory,

Who Was the Enemy?

Just east of Salt Lake City, Fort Douglas stands as a reminder of Utah's early days. The fort was built in 1863 by Colonel Patrick Edward Connor. At that time, the Civil War was raging, and there was also warfare between the settlers and Indians. Allegedly, Fort Douglas was established to protect the settlers and to guard the telegraph line that connected California with Union cities in the East. But some historians believe the fort also allowed the U.S. military to keep an eye on Mormon activity. Today the fort contains a museum on military activities in Utah. Exhibits include maps and drawings from the Escalante expedition, rifles used by the U.S. Army during the Utah War, and photos and memorabilia of military installations of the twentieth century. The cemetery on the grounds of the fort has gravestones dating back to the 1860s. ∎

their saddlebags bulging with mail. Suddenly a letter could travel from Salt Lake City to Washington, D.C., in only seven days. Then, in October 1861, a telegraph line spanned the nation and the Pony Express was obsolete. Suddenly coded messages leaped across the miles in an instant. In 1869, the nation's first transcontinental railroad was completed at Promontory Point. Trains brought goods to Utah and carried Utah's produce to markets east and west. The trains also brought new settlers to Utah Territory. Some were Mormons. But there were also New England Yankees, Irish Catholics, Pennsylvania

America's first transcontinental railroad was completed in 1869 at Promontory Point.

Plural Wife

Ann Eliza Webb was born in Nauvoo, Illinois, and raised in the Mormon faith. After traveling west along the Mormon Trail, she married Brigham Young and became one of his twenty-seven wives. Ann Eliza found life as a "plural wife" to be thanklessly hard. Eventually she fled from Lion House, the Salt Lake City home she shared with several of Young's other wives and their children, and sued Young for divorce. Her case won national notoriety.

After Ann Eliza Young left Utah, she traveled throughout the country lecturing on the evils of polygamy. Her story fueled opposition to the Mormons and spurred Congress to pass strong antipolygamy laws. In her 1878 autobiography, *Wife No. 19*, Young writes: "I have consecrated myself to the work, not merely for my own sake, but for the sake of all the unhappy women of Utah, who, unlike myself, are either too powerless or too timid to break the fetters which bind them." ■

Wilford Woodruff recommended that Mormons give up polygamy.

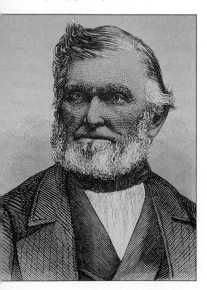

Germans, and people from many other backgrounds. Many of these Gentiles came to mine gold, copper, and other valuable minerals. Mormon influence remained strong in Utah, but other voices clamored to be heard.

In 1890, yielding to pressure from federal officials, Mormon Church president Wilford Woodruff advised the Mormons to give up polygamy. It was prohibited by the church after 1904. This proclamation led to a period of turmoil in Utah. Some Mormon men chose one wife and abandoned the others. Some continued to live as before, with all of their wives and children. Many Mormons felt that Woodruff's proclamation was merely designed to appease the federal government. They went to Canada or Mexico to perform plural marriages because the practice was forbidden in the United States.

Gold in the Mountains

In 1862, the U.S. Army sent Colonel Patrick Edward Connor (1820–1891) to enforce federal laws against polygamy in Utah. After defeating the Shoshone in the 1863 Bear River Massacre, in Idaho, Connor was hailed as a hero and rose to the rank of general. But Connor was not especially concerned with his mission to end plural marriage. His chief interest was mining, and in Utah he threw himself into a quest for valuable minerals. Connor encouraged exploration for gold, silver, copper, and other metals in Utah's mountains. His work brought Gentiles pouring into Utah with picks and shovels, intent on making their fortunes. Thanks to his efforts, gold was discovered in Bingham Canyon in the 1870s, and Utah's mining industry became highly profitable. ■

Woodruff's announcement had one clear positive result. It paved the way for Congress to grant statehood to Utah Territory. Utah's bid for statehood was finally accepted in 1895. On January 4, 1896, President Grover Cleveland proclaimed Utah the forty-fifth state of the United States.

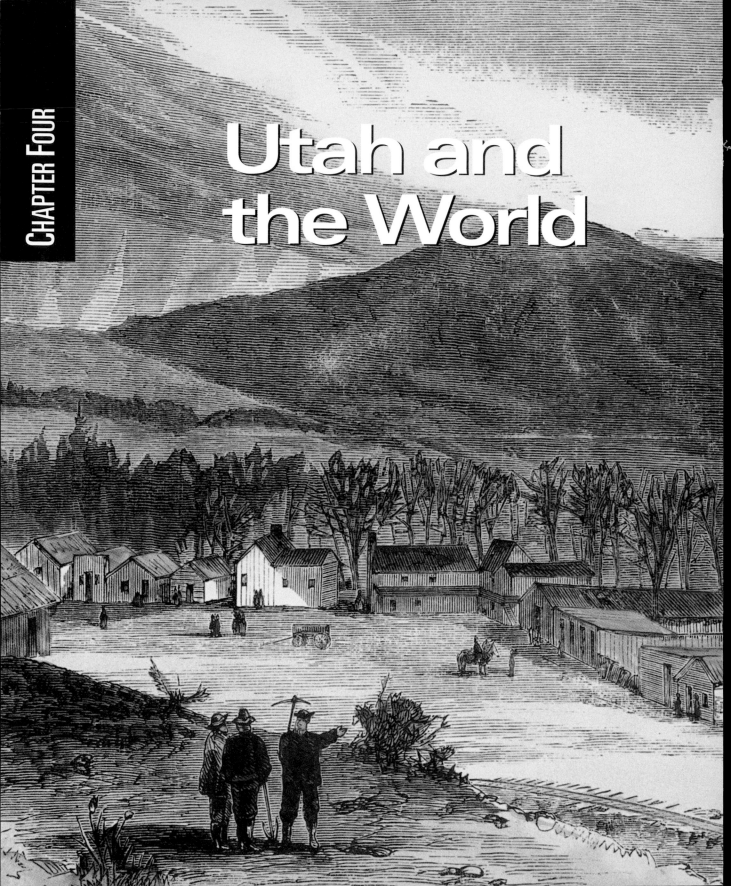

CHAPTER FOUR

Utah and the World

In 1898, two years after Utah became a state, Utahns elected Brigham H. Roberts to represent them in Congress. Roberts, who held a prominent place in the Mormon Church, had several wives. Public opinion swelled against Mormonism and polygamy. More than a million Americans signed a petition demanding that Roberts not be seated. At last the House of Representatives voted not to admit Roberts to its ranks.

During its early years of statehood, Utah remained isolated from the rest of the United States. Many Americans still regarded Mormonism as strange and unlawful. During the twentieth century, Utah gradually moved into the mainstream. But it has never lost a character all its own.

Brigham H. Roberts was denied admission to Congress in 1898.

Joining the Battle

The Mormons in general had been opposed to slavery. But when the Civil War broke out in 1861, few Utahns enlisted in the Union army. Utahns felt far removed from the conflict that ravaged the states to the east. Utah reacted very differently, however, when the United States went to war with Spain in 1898. Eager to prove its patriotism, Utah sent three batteries of artillery and two cavalry units to fight in Cuba and the Philippines.

In 1903, Utahns again faced public outcry when they elected a

Opposite: The Union Pacific Railroad at Echo City

Reed Smoot served in the Senate until 1933.

Mormon leader, Reed Smoot, to serve in the Senate. Smoot spent the next four years fighting for his seat. At last the furor subsided and Smoot was accepted as a full-fledged member of the Senate. He served until 1933, leaving a distinguished record of legislation behind him.

By 1900, Utahns had turned thousands of dry acres into farmland. By channeling water from lakes, rivers, and streams, they brought life to once-barren hillsides and valleys. In about 1912, many Utahns turned to a technique called dry farming in which fields were left unplanted every other year. In this way, enough moisture built up in the land to support wheat, barley, and other crops during the alternate years.

Despite the success of dry farming, vast expanses of land were still too parched to support crops. Then in 1913, the U.S. Bureau of Land Reclamation completed the Strawberry River Reservoir. The reservoir was the first of several large-scale engineering efforts that helped to water Utah's deserts. Increased irrigation also helped to expand Utah's rangeland, aiding the development of the cattle industry.

In 1917, the United States entered World War I (1914–1918), a conflict that had already raged in Europe for three years. Some 21,000 Utahns put on uniforms to take part in the war effort. Before the fighting was over, 760 Utahns lost their lives. The state's mines provided copper and other minerals needed in the manufacture of

Putting the Cows on the Mountain

Every spring, Utah ranchers roped and branded calves. The cattle were then herded by cowboys to open grazing land, where they would fatten on grasses all through the summer. This practice was known as "taking the cows to the mountain."

In October it was time to "bring the cows off the mountain" and ship them to market. Cowboys in overalls and broad Stetson hats lassoed the fat, feisty cattle and herded them to railway depots. Often a truck carried food and other supplies, but most of the actual herding was done by cowboys until the 1940s. ■

weapons. Utah's wholehearted support of the war effort demonstrated how fully it had become part of the United States.

Rich Times and Hard Times

After World War I, the U.S. economy boomed. The nation hungered for fuel to heat homes and power factories. Utah's coal mines and natural gas fields went into high gear. Copper mines, too, increased

Perjury Farm

A few Utah farmers experimented with dry farming, or planting fields without irrigation, as early as 1863. But most Utahns doubted that dry farming could succeed. In the 1880s, David Broadhead, a farmer from Nephi, told a court that he could grow wheat without irrigation. The court indicted him for perjury, or lying under oath. Broadhead went on to become one of the leading wheat growers in the state, all without irrigating his fields. Proudly he hung a sign on his gate that read PERJURY FARM. ■

The Ballad of Joe Hill

In 1915, a Swedish immigrant named Joe Hill (1879–1915) was executed by a firing squad in Salt Lake City. Hill was sentenced to death for the murder of a shop-keeper, but the evidence against him was strictly circumstantial. Many people believed that Hill was framed because of his involvement with coal-miners' unions in Utah.

Hill was born Joel Hagglund in a small town in Sweden. After emi-grating to the United States, he wandered through the West, work-ing an assortment of jobs and writ-ing songs in his spare time. In 1910, he joined the International Workers of the World (IWW), a rad-ical labor organization that sought to give power to the workers. Many of his songs carried the IWW's message.

When Hill was sentenced to die, protests arose all over America. Even President Woodrow Wilson asked that his life be spared. But the governor of Utah refused to pardon Joe Hill. With his death, Hill became a martyr for the cause of labor. He is still regarded as an American folk hero. ■

their output to meet new demand. Railroads and mining had brought the first non-Mormon immigrants to Utah back in the nineteenth century, and as the twentieth century rolled forward, Gentiles continued moving into the state. Rural areas remained loyal to old Mormon traditions, but Salt Lake City gracefully accepted the new diversity.

As Utahns grew more willing to accept outsiders, they discovered a vigorous new industry—tourism. By the 1920s, a network of highways brought some of the state's stunning natural wonders within reach of visitors. A colorful brochure, printed in 1929, invited sightseers to the Canyonlands in southeastern Utah. The map led tourists along a series of highways with such picturesque names as Arrow Head Trail, Navajo Trail, and the Old Mormon Trail. Utah was turning its frontier history into hard cash.

Even in these prosperous times, however, Utah faced economic hardships. During the 1920s, the price of wheat, corn, and other farm products fell sharply. Many Utah farmers were forced to sell their land and move to Salt Lake City, Ogden, Provo, or other towns. Furthermore, the nation's biggest markets were on the Atlantic and Pacific Coasts. Utah, locked behind formidable mountains and deserts, lay far from either of these major population centers. To send their produce to profitable markets, Utah farmers depended on the railroads. But the railroad companies charged exorbitant fees for this service, taking a huge bite out of the farmers' final earnings.

In 1929, prices crashed on the stock exchange in New York City. The stock-market crash thrust the United States into a terrible business slump call the Great Depression. Utah was hit especially hard. As factories closed around the country, Utah's mining industry collapsed. To make matters worse, severe drought struck the state in 1931 and 1932. Farmers who had barely been surviving were now driven to bankruptcy. Many families in rural areas could not afford running water, electricity, or telephone service.

New railroads enabled Utah's farmers to send their produce to market, but at a high cost.

Mining was a booming business during World War II.

Life for them had changed little since the Mormon pioneers crossed the plains nearly a century earlier.

In December 1941, Japanese planes bombed the U.S. Navy fleet at Pearl Harbor, Hawaii, and the United States entered World War II (1939–1945). Almost overnight, factories reopened to churn out weapons, tanks, and uniforms. The surge in demand for raw minerals revived mining in Utah. Prices for beef and produce rose too. Army installations opened near Salt Lake City and at Brigham City and Ogden. The war brought prosperity to Utah once more, but it took the lives of thousands of Utah soldiers who served in Europe and the Pacific. Prosperity came at a terrible cost.

Winds of Change

As a small child in 1957, Terry Tempest Williams was riding home with her family along a highway in western Utah. Suddenly her parents noticed a mysterious light in the sky. Years later Williams remembered that strange incident: "We all got out of the car and watched this golden-stemmed mushroom cloud rising from the

Fighting for the Land

Terry Tempest Williams (1955–) grew up near Salt Lake City in a devout Mormon family. When one relative after another died of cancer, she became convinced that radiation and toxic chemicals were to blame. Williams launched a crusade for a healthier environment. When a bill proposed to open 20 million acres (8 million ha) in southern Utah to commercial development, Williams organized a campaign of resistance. She and eighteen other Utah writers created a book of essays about the region's unique natural beauty and gave a copy to every member of Congress. The bill was tabled (put aside and never voted on) in 1996. ■

desert floor." Williams and her family had witnessed the test blast of an atomic bomb in Nevada, just across the Utah line. Between 1951 and 1962, the U.S. military regularly tested atomic weapons in the deserts of Utah and Nevada. This arid, treeless country seemed the perfect place for developing weapons of mass destruction.

When the military began to test nuclear weapons in the early 1950s, no one knew the long-term effects of radioactive fallout on human beings. Years later, many people who lived downwind from

Nuclear testing took place in the deserts of Nevada and Utah during the 1950s and 1960s.

the blasts developed cancer. During the 1980s, groups of citizens sought the truth about the tests and their impact on people in the region. In 1991, the federal government compensated some 1,100 "downwinders" in Utah, Nevada, and Arizona for health problems caused by exposure to radiation. But questions still remain about the government's tests of these weapons.

A key ingredient in the production of nuclear weapons was a radioactive mineral called uranium. In 1952, rich deposits of uranium were found near the town of Moab. The discovery brought engineers, miners, and investors rushing to Utah. In the atomic age, uranium was more precious than gold.

The Silent Killer

On March 14, 1968, 6,400 sheep in Tooele County, Utah, collapsed and died in the fields where they grazed. Ranchers in the area believed the sheep had died because of a weapons test gone awry. For four years, the ranchers demanded the truth, but the government gave no direct answers. Then, in 1972, secret government records were revealed to the public. The sheep had been killed by nerve gas that was being tested at nearby Dugway Proving Ground. The wind had changed unexpectedly, carrying the gas to the flocks of sheep.

Most Utahns staunchly support the military. But the Tooele County disaster awakened deep concern among many Utah citizens. In the 1990s, the U.S. Army announced plans to destroy 13,000 tons of toxic chemicals that were stored in bunkers on Utah's soil. Some of the bunkers had begun to leak. Utahns worried that these chemicals could spill or disperse on the wind if they were moved. Such fears heightened when the army began to incinerate the chemicals at a plant near Tooele. Utah's stored chemical weapons present an ongoing dilemma. ■

In the second half of the twentieth century, Utah was one of the last states in the nation with vast tracts of undeveloped land. As its population increased, questions arose as to how the state's land should be used. Mining companies hoped to exploit Utah's reserves of coal, natural gas, petroleum, and other minerals. They promised that expanded mining would create jobs in underdeveloped rural

Uranium mining southeast of Moab

The Grand Staircase-Escalante National Monument is off-limits to mining and other development.

areas. Business entrepreneurs drew plans for ski resorts that would lure vacationers with money to spend. Environmentalists fought to preserve Utah's unspoiled wilderness for future generations. Some Utahns often felt that environmentalists were meddling outsiders who did not respect their interests and needs.

President Bill Clinton brought the land-use controversy to a head in the fall of 1996. Without even discussing his plans with

Utah's governor and members of Congress, he designated 1.8 million acres (729,000 ha) of land in southern Utah as the Grand Staircase-Escalante National Monument. Under this ruling, mining would be banned in all undeveloped areas within the area. Rural residents who wanted the land for mining protested by entering the monument with bulldozers and carving roads to nowhere, simply to prove that development had already begun. Townspeople in Kanab, at the edge of the protected land, sent up a cloud of black balloons. Utahns were especially upset because they were never consulted about the project. "I feel like I'm back in the 1850s again," said Utah Congressman Chris Cannon, "with the federal government encamped all around us."

Eventually, however, most Utahns accepted and even welcomed President Clinton's decree. The Grand Staircase region is stunningly beautiful, containing rock formations unlike those anywhere else on Earth. And, once lost, it can never be replaced. It is one of the many utterly spectacular natural features of this remarkable state.

CHAPTER FIVE

The Land Nobody Wanted

"**W**hat a world of grandeur is spread before us! Below is the canyon through which the Colorado runs. We can trace its route for miles, and at points catch glimpses of the river. From the northwest comes the Green in a narrow winding gorge. From the northeast comes the Grand, through a canyon that seems bottomless from where we stand. Away to the west are lines of cliff and ledges of rock, . . . ledges from which the gods might quarry mountains. Rolled out on the plain below would stand a lofty range, . . . cliffs where the soaring eagle is lost to view ere he reaches the summit. . . . Wherever we look there is but a wilderness of rocks, deep gorges where the rivers are lost below cliffs, and towers and pinnacles and ten thousand strangely carved forms in every direction; and beyond them mountains blending with the clouds."

John Wesley Powell

—From the journal of John Wesley Powell, 1869, written at Grand View Point in present-day Canyonlands National Park

The Beautiful Wasteland

When Brigham Young set out with the first Mormon band from Nauvoo, Illinois, he hoped to find a land that no one else wanted. With its forbidding mountain chains and lonesome deserts, Utah was precisely what he sought. Today towns and cities nestle among

Opposite: Virgin River, Zion National Park

the mountains, and cars stream across the desert along four-lane highways. But Utah has not lost its sense of wildness and mystery. It is still a land unlike any other.

Utah lies almost midway between Canada and Mexico in the Rocky Mountain region of the United States. On a map, the state forms a perfect rectangle with a second, smaller oblong extending from its northwestern corner. Utah is bordered by Arizona to the south, Nevada to the west, Idaho and Wyoming to the north, and Colorado to the east. At the southeastern corner, the boundaries of four states come together—Utah, Colorado, Arizona, and New Mexico. This is the only place in the nation where four states meet. Utah has an area of 84,905 square miles (219,904 sq km), including 2,736 square miles (7,086 sq km) of inland water. Among the fifty states, Utah ranks thirteenth in size.

Utah's Geographical Features

Total area; rank	84,905 sq. mi. (219,904 sq km); 13th
Land; rank	82,169 sq. mi. (212,818 sq km); 12th
Water; rank	2,736 sq. mi. (7,086 sq km); 14th
Inland water; rank	2,736 sq. mi (7,086 sq km); 7th
Geographic center	Sanpete, 3 miles (4.8 km) north of Manti
Highest point	Kings Peak, 13,528 feet (4,126 m)
Lowest point	Beaverdam Creek in Washington County, 2,000 feet (610 m)
Largest city	Salt Lake City
Population; rank	1,727,784 (1990 census); 35th
Record high temperature	116°F (47°C) at St. George on June 28, 1892
Record low temperature	–50°F (–46°C) at Woodruff on February 6, 1899, and in Utah County on January 5, 1913
Average July temperature	73°F (23°C)
Average January temperature	25°F (–4°C)
Average annual precipitation	12 inches (30 cm)

The Rocky Mountains consist of a series of mountain ranges stretching north to south through Canada and the western United States. Utah is crossed by two of these ranges, the Wasatch and the Uinta. Running from Utah's northern boundary southward to the middle of the state, the Wasatch Range is very ancient in origin. These mountains contain some of the oldest rocks geologists have ever found, dating back 2 billion years. The Uintas are the only range in the Rockies that runs east to west instead of north to south. Kings Peak, the highest point in the state at 13,528 feet (4,126 m), stands in the Uinta Range.

South of these mountains the land tumbles downward through a series of plateaus and lower mountain ranges. In southeastern Utah, the land is fractured into a maze of deep, jagged canyons and towering rock formations that look like they were made by a sculptor from Jupiter. In 1861, the *Deseret News* described this region as "measurably valueless, excepting for . . . hunting grounds for Indians, and to hold the world together."

The Wasatch Mountain Range crosses the state.

This region, which seemed so useless to the pioneers, contains some of the most spectacular natural formations on Earth. Wind and water erosion have carved great standing rocks into arches, spires, and natural bridges. Flat vertical rocks, like dinner plates standing on edge, are known as fins. One geologist refers to Utah as the "Bedrock State," because so many layers of bedrock are exposed in its cliffs. These layers are visible where the cliffs change color, from pink to white to gray to vermilion.

Mesa Arch, one of the many natural rock formations found in Utah

Preserving a Natural Heritage

Millions of acres of land in Utah are preserved in their natural state for future generations. Utah has five national parks, seven national monuments, and forty-four state parks. The Grand Staircase-Escalante National Monument, created in 1996, is more than twice the size of Rhode Island. The Grand Staircase is a remarkable rock formation whose "steps" are 900 feet (275 m) high. ■

About 25,000 years ago, western Utah was covered by a vast body of water that geologists call Lake Bonneville. As the lake receded, it left behind an immense depression known as the Great Basin. The last traces of Lake Bonneville are Utah Lake and Great Salt Lake. The Bonneville Salt Flats cover about 70 square miles (181 sq km). The soil is so salty that no plants can grow there and so level that one can observe the curvature of the earth by gazing at the horizon.

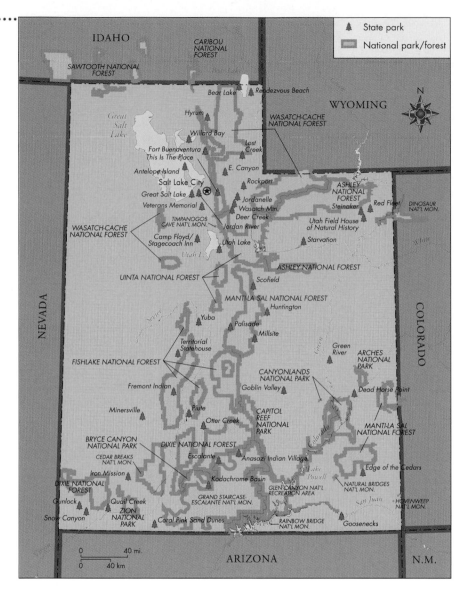

Utah's parks and forests

Though much of Utah's land is very dry, the state has many rivers. The Colorado and many of its winding branches flow through Utah east of the Wasatch Range. The Bear, Weber, and Provo Rivers flow west from the Uinta Range. The longest river in south-central Utah is the Sevier. Raft River cuts across Utah's northwest corner and eventually flows into the Snake River in Idaho.

Where the Wild Things Are

About 30 percent of Utah is covered with forests. Most of the forests are in the state's mountainous regions. The stately ponderosa pine stretches to a height of 150 feet (46 m). The hardy piñon pine is smaller and can survive at higher altitudes. Sycamores grow along the banks of rivers and streams, while the quaking aspen shivers from base to crown in the slightest breeze.

West of the Wasatch Range, in the Great Basin, the plant life changes dramatically. Trees disappear, replaced by grasses and low bushes. The common sagebrush is a tangled bush that grows 3 to 6 feet (1 to 2 m) high. Transplanted Utahns feel homesick when they remember the sharp smell of sagebrush on the breeze.

Part of the Colorado River winds through Utah.

The Inland Sea

Utah's Great Salt Lake is the largest salt lake in North America and one of the biggest in the world. The lake's size changes continually and has ranged from 1,000 square miles (2,590 sq km) to 2,300 square miles (5,957 sq km). During the 1990s, the lake's waters steadily receded. Great Salt Lake is fed by three rivers—Bear, Weber, and Jordan—and has no outlet. The water gets its extremely high salt content from the soil of the Great Basin.

The salty water can be unpleasant at first, but if the salt level is high and the water level is low, swimmers enjoy an unusual ability to float. Writer Terry Tempest Williams describes her childhood visits: "The ritual was always the same. Run into the lake, scream, and run back out. The salt seeped into the sores on our scraped knees and lingered. And if the stinging sensation didn't bring you to tears, the brine flies did. We begged [Mother] to take us home, pleading for dry towels. Total time at the lake: five minutes. She was unsympathetic. 'We're here for the afternoon, kids,' she said. . . . 'I didn't see anyone floating.' She had given us a dare. One by one, we slowly entered Great Salt Lake. Gradually, we would lean backward into the hands of the cool water and find ourselves being held by the very lake that minutes before had betrayed us. For hours we floated on our backs, imprinting on Great Basin skies." ■

Utah's forests and canyons are home to many animals, large and small. Visitors are thrilled to view elk, mule deer, and pronghorn. Small herds of bison are protected in designated areas of parks and national monuments. Coyotes thrive from remote canyon country to the outskirts of Salt Lake City. Jackrabbits, twice the size of the common eastern cottontail, can often be seen loping along beside the highways. Far more shy are badgers, weasels, and bobcats. Campers should beware of marauding black bears attracted to food supplies and garbage. Mountain lions, or cougars, usually

Pronghorn antelopes are among the many animals found in Utah.

River Wild

The foaming rapids of the Green and Colorado Rivers have such colorful names as Bin Hurt, Ten Cent, and Disaster Falls. Many of these rapids were christened by geologist John Wesley Powell (1834–1902), who explored the Colorado and its tributaries in the late 1860s and 1870s. Powell made careful studies of Utah's rock formations. In addition, he studied the languages and traditions of the Ute and Paiute.

Powell fought in the Civil War and lost his right arm at the Battle of Shiloh. For the rest of his life he was known as Major Powell. He was not only a scientist but also a talented writer. In his books and journals, he captures the beauty and excitement of travel in Utah's wild places. ■

avoid human beings, but occasionally they are known to kill sheep or calves.

Bald eagles can sometimes be sighted as they drift on air currents high overhead, searching the ground for prey. Several species of hawks and owls are also found in the state. Ducks and geese nest on the lakes and rivers. Shorebirds including gulls, plovers, and sandpipers nest in the marshes around Great Salt Lake. The lake also serves as a resting place for migrating shorebirds.

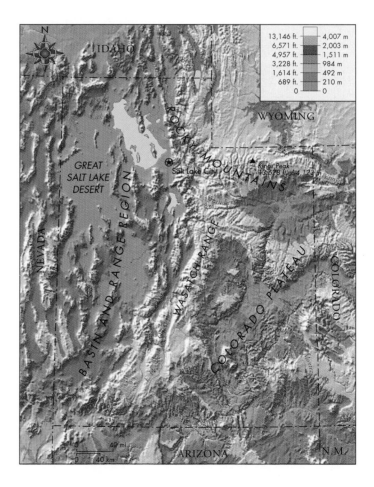

Topographical map of Utah

One of Utah's most unusual birds is the roadrunner (made famous by the popular cartoon character). A member of the cuckoo family, the roadrunner is a weak flier and prefers to stride along the ground. It is a fierce hunter and is not afraid to tackle the deadly rattlesnake. Utah has several species of rattlers, including the diamondback and the sidewinder. The sidewinder moves by throwing its body sideways in a graceful loop. Its track in the desert looks like a series of *S*'s.

When Giants Walked the Earth

Outside the town of Vernal stands the 60-foot (18-m) cement cast of the skeleton of a diplodocus, an immense plant-eating dinosaur whose skeleton was excavated in northeastern Utah. Utah is rich in traces of dinosaurs, creatures that have been extinct for 65 million years. Utah's unique rock formations expose many strata, or layers, created in different geological periods. Under these conditions, fossils are relatively easy to find. At Dinosaur National Monument, visitors can watch scientists as they search for bones, painstakingly chipping them from surrounding stone. ■

Trout, catfish, whitefish, perch, and bass live in Utah's rivers and freshwater lakes. The only creatures that can live in the waters of the Great Salt Lake are tiny crustaceans called brine shrimp. These small shellfish are an excellent source of food for the birds that live around the lake.

Under the Weather

Climate varies widely in Utah, depending upon the altitude and the region. The lowest parts of the state, the Santa Clara and Virgin River Valleys, have an altitude of about 2,700 feet (824 m). These valleys have been nicknamed "Utah's Dixie" because of their mild temperatures. By contrast, high in the Wasatch Range and Uinta Mountains, summers are short and the long winters are harsh and stormy. Travelers are warned that snow slides can occur on mountain roads from late October until early June.

Not surprisingly, Brigham Young established his first settlements along the western side of Utah's Wasatch Range, commonly called the Wasatch Front. This part of the state receives the most rainfall, as much as 50 inches (127 centimeters) per year. It was relatively easy to turn the raw land there into productive fields. By contrast, the deserts of southwestern Utah are bone-dry with an annual precipitation of only 5 inches (13 cm). Snowfall is virtually unknown in the desert. But the mountains around Salt Lake City may be buried under 400 inches (1,016 cm) of snow a year.

The average January temperature in northeastern Utah is 20° Fahrenheit (−7° Celsius), compared with 39°F (4°C) in the southwestern corner of the state. July temperatures in the northeast average 60°F (16°C), while the average July reading in the south-

Bird of the Rushing Streams

In appearance, there is nothing unusual about the dipper, or water ouzel. It is a small, grayish bird with a stubby tail. But the dipper has an extraordinary lifestyle. It walks along the bottoms of rushing streams, snatching insects as they whiz by. It will even plunge fearlessly into rapids and waterfalls. Underwater, the dipper uses its wings as paddles. ∎

west is 84°F (29°C). In the desert, the mercury often soars above the 100°F (38°C). The hottest temperature in Utah history was 116°F (47°C), recorded at St. George on June 28, 1892. On two occasions temperatures of –50°F (–46°C) have been documented—at Woodruff on February 6, 1899, and in Utah County on January 5, 1913.

Snowfall in Big Cotton-wood Canyon

CHAPTER SIX

Utah East and West

Brigham Young laid out Salt Lake City on a precise grid pattern. Its streets still follow the careful numbering system Young devised. They radiate to north and south, east and west, with Temple Square as their hub. Other Utah cities and towns were modeled on Salt Lake City. Wherever you travel in Utah, these towns with their neat square blocks are reminders of the state's founders. Yet Utah has undergone tremendous changes since Brigham Young arrived. As you explore the state, you will find evidence of those changes all around you.

Overlooking the city of St. George

Towns of the South

Southern Utah is a sparsely populated land where nature makes the rules. Towns are small and widely scattered through the state's scenic canyon country. Visitors pour in to enjoy the national parks, but not many people live in this region year-round.

The largest city in southern Utah is St. George, near Zion National Park in the southwestern corner of the state. The town was named for its founder, George A. Smith. According to Brigham Young, Smith was one of those holy leaders who could be called a Latter-day Saint. St. George is dominated by a magnificent white Mormon temple.

Opposite: Snow Canyon Recreational Area

St. George is known for this large Mormon temple.

Utahns sometimes say that St. George is "where the sun spends the winter." Because of its gentle climate, the city has developed as a thriving winter resort. Visitors from colder climes enjoy its golf courses, tennis courts, and elegant restaurants.

In rural southern Utah, Cedar City is an oasis of culture. Home to Southern Utah University, Cedar City hosts dozens of concerts, dance events, and a Shakespeare Festival each year. A pioneer exhibit in Iron Mission State Park features antique farm equipment, buggies, wagons, and stagecoaches. One stagecoach is riddled with bullet holes from an attack by the famous outlaw known as Butch Cassidy.

Founded by Mormons in 1870, the little town of Kanab never had a chance to grow. The impassable canyon of the Colorado River sent railroads and wagon trains far to the north. Then, in 1924, Hollywood discovered that Kanab was a perfect setting for western movies. More than fifty films have been made in Kanab, including John Wayne's 1949 hit *She Wore a Yellow Ribbon* and the 1962 box-office smash *How the West Was Won*.

Blanding, in the southeastern corner of the state, is surrounded by the ruins of Anasazi culture. The White Mesa Institute houses an intriguing collection of Native American artifacts from prehistoric times, as well as crafts of the Ute and Paiute. Special programs

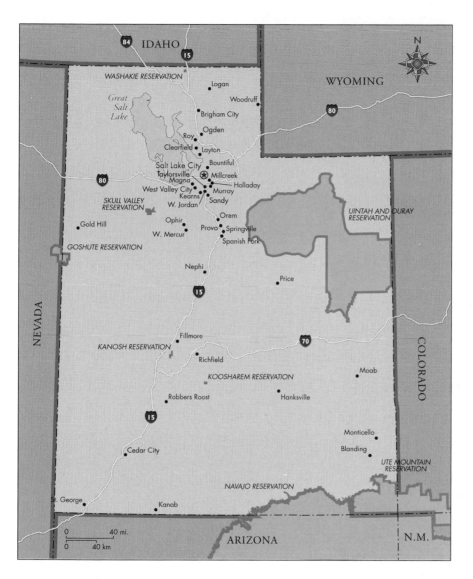

IDAHO

84

15

WASHAKIE RESERVATION

Logan

Great Salt Lake

Woodruff

Brigham City

Ogden

Roy

Clearfield • Layton

Bountiful

Salt Lake City
Taylorsville ⊛ Millcreek
Magna Holladay
West Valley City Murray
Kearns Sandy
W. Jordan

WYOMING

80

80

SKULL VALLEY RESERVATION

Gold Hill

Ophir
W. Mercur

Orem

Provo • Springville
Spanish Fork

GOSHUTE RESERVATION

UINTAH AND OURAY RESERVATION

NEVADA

Nephi

Price

15

Fillmore

KANOSH RESERVATION

Richfield

70

KOOSHAREM RESERVATION

Moab

COLORADO

Robbers Roost

Hanksville

15

Monticello

Cedar City

Blanding

UTE MOUNTAIN RESERVATION

NAVAJO RESERVATION

St. George

Kanab

0   40 mi.

0   40 km

ARIZONA

N.M.

Utah's cities and interstates

focus on such topics as Indian dances, games, and legends. Other exhibits on Anasazi culture can be seen at the Cedars Museum.

Monticello was founded in 1887 by five pioneering Mormon families. Their leader had the improbable name of Parley Butt. In 1892, the quiet Mormon settlement was rocked by the discovery of

Monticello Lake at the base of the Abajo Mountains

gold in the surrounding Abajo Mountains. Prospectors rushed into town, eager to stake claims and spend what money they had. Most were soon disappointed, and Monticello became a sleepy little town again.

Historians believe that Escalante and Dominguez, the early Spanish explorers, entered Utah somewhere near present-day Moab. Moab made history again in 1952, when valuable deposits of uranium were discovered nearby. Moab lies in some of the most spectacular country of southeastern Utah, within easy driving distance of Canyonlands and Arches National Parks. To the southwest spreads Behind-the-Rocks, some 50 square miles (130 sq km) of canyons, arches, and mesas.

Behind-the-Rocks, a magnificent collection of arches, mesas, and canyons

Price was named for a Mormon bishop, William Price, who led an exploring party through the region in 1869. Just south of Price is the Cleveland-Lloyd Dinosaur Quarry, one of the most productive fossil sites in the state. Teams of scientists can usually be seen at work there. At the College of Eastern Utah's Prehistoric Museum at Price, many fossils from the region are on display, including dinosaur footprints and the skeleton of a mammoth. The skeleton of a 30-foot (9.2-m) allosaurus, a fierce meat-eating dinosaur, greets visitors to Price's city hall.

The Wasatch Front

The western third of Utah is a desert landscape, almost empty of human communities. Here and there, mining towns have sprung up, often fading away when the ore is exhausted. Such towns as Ophir,

Robbers Roost

In the late nineteenth century, the country between Hanksville and Moab was known as Robbers Roost. Its rocky canyons provided hideaways for outlaws who stole cattle, robbed banks, and held up stagecoaches. Best remembered of these "bad guys" was Butch Cassidy, born Robert Leroy Parker. According to legend, Cassidy was a kind of American Robin Hood who stole from the rich and gave to the poor. In one story, he robbed a bank and gave the money to a poor widow who could not pay the mortgage on her home. When the banker came to put her off the land, she paid everything she owed. As the banker rode back to town, Cassidy held him up and took back the money! ■

Gold Hill, and Mercury are lonely dots in this vast expanse. Most of the state's cities and towns cluster along the Wasatch Front, along the western base of the Wasatch Range. Ogden, at the northern end of this metropolitan area, lies on the Ogden and Weber Rivers. Pleasant parks line the Ogden River, which winds through the center of town. Ben Lomond Peak, which overshadows the town, is familiar to moviegoers as part of the logo of Paramount Pictures.

Ogden was named after Peter Skene Ogden, one of Utah's most famous mountain men. The town got a major boost in 1869 with the completion of the transcontinental railroad. Then, in 1939, Hill Air Force Base opened south of town, bringing thousands of servicemen and their families. One of Ogden's attractions is the Hill Air Force Base Museum, where visitors can see generations of aircraft and related artifacts. The Union Station Museum recalls Ogden's railroad days with a collection of engines and other train memorabilia. This museum also pays tribute to the life and work of firearms inventor John Browning.

Union Station in Ogden

On the last Friday of July, some 50,000 people flock to Logan for the eight-day Festival of the American West. The festival celebrates Utah's frontier heritage with food, music, storytelling, and local crafts, many made by Native Americans. Visitors can march into an army camp, watch a Wild West show, and even pan for gold.

Just southwest of Logan is the Jensen Living Historical Farm. This unique museum gives visitors a hands-on experience of Utah farm life in about 1917, allowing them to help plant wheat, harvest corn, milk cows, or can fresh vegetables. The museum serves as a training ground for agriculture students and for women and men who plan to work in museums and parks throughout the country.

Brigham Young University was founded in Provo in 1875.

John Browning

Guns were a way of life in frontier Utah. But for John Browning (1855–1926), growing up beside his father's gun shop in Ogden, they became an obsession. Browning designed his first rifle when he was only thirteen. Later he developed an assortment of rifles that were marketed by such companies as Colt and Winchester. In 1918, the U.S. Army adopted the Browning automatic rifle, known as the BAR, for regular use. The BAR and other Browning weapons were used throughout World War II and remained in service until the late 1950s. ■

Provo is home to Brigham Young University, founded in 1875. The city is also headquarters for several fast-growing companies in the world of computer technology. One of Provo's more unique attractions is the McCurdy Historical Doll Museum, with its collection of more than 3,000 dolls from around the globe. Adjoining the museum is a doll hospital where broken dolls are repaired. The Pioneer Memorial Museum includes the exact replica of a Mormon pioneer cabin from the 1850s.

The Capital City

The planners of Salt Lake City's intended it to be Utah's crowning jewel. The city, which serves as the state capital, is also the hub of Utah's economy and culture. Salt Lake City is by far the largest city in the state, and its outlying suburbs are growing rapidly.

Like most U.S. cities, Salt Lake City is ringed with shopping malls and fast-food restaurants. But the city's core has an unmistakable character that reflects its deeply honored traditions. Utahns place great value on education, and Salt Lake's libraries and muse-

Salt Lake City is the state's center of culture and finance.

ums offer a wealth of opportunities for learning. Visitors to Hansen Planetarium can take in laser light shows, films, and lectures on the heavens. The Salt Lake City Children's Museum provides kids with a host of novel experiences. You can try simulated flight in a Boeing 727, dig up the skeleton of a saber-toothed cat, or walk among the hammers and strings of a giant piano. At Tracy Aviary, get a close-up look at such birds as the bald eagle and the startling, exotic hyacinthine macaw. Red Butte Garden, east of the city near Fort Douglas, includes an arboretum with a stunning variety of trees and a conservatory with desert and rain-forest habitats.

The University of Utah stands on a "bench" or plateau beneath the Wasatch Range just east of the city. Throughout the year, the university enriches the cultural life of the region. The Utah Museum of Fine Arts, located on the university campus, has a fine collection of paintings and sculpture. Ancient Egypt, Renaissance Italy, Asia, Africa, and the United States are all well represented. The Utah Museum of Natural History has displays on western wildlife, Native American cultures, and Utah minerals.

The Trapper from Canada

The city of Provo and the Provo River bear the name of French Canadian trapper Etienne Provost. Very little is known about Provost's life. In 1824, he entered Utah from the north with a band of trappers sent by Captain William Ashley. Some historians believe that Provost, rather than Jim Bridger, may have been the first white person to see Great Salt Lake. Others argue that the honor belongs to Peter Skene Ogden. But nobody will ever know for sure. ■

Salt Lake City is touched by all the problems that occur in most of urban America, including drug use and gang warfare. Some people are homeless. But in general the city is clean, safe, and prosperous. The mansions along South Temple Street are reminders of the great wealth that has flowed into the city over the years. The twenty-eight-room Kearns Mansion was built by mining magnate Thomas Kearns. Kearns founded the *Salt Lake City Tribune*, Utah's largest newspaper. The Kearns Mansion is the official home of Utah's governor.

At the heart of Salt Lake City is the 10-acre (4-ha) walled plaza known as Temple Square. Nearby stands Beehive House, once the home of Brigham Young. The sculpted beehive on the roof is a symbol of Mormon industry and community. Adjacent to Beehive House is Lion House, where Young died. Several of Young's twenty-seven wives lived at Lion House with their children. Not far away, the headquarters of the Mormon Church is housed in a modern twenty-eight-story tower. West of Temple Square are buildings containing the Museum of Church History and Art and the Mormon Family History Library.

Every hour, a great bronze bell rings out over Temple

Lion House, one of Brigham Young's homes

Viewing the Temple

It is not easy to be admitted to the Salt Lake Temple. You must present documents to prove you are an active member of the Mormon Church and show a recommendation from your bishop. Such recommendations are given only to Mormons in good standing with the church. Non-Mormons are not permitted to set foot in the temple itself under any circumstances. But they can take a "mini-tour" of the temple at either of the two visitors' centers on Temple Square. The centers offer replicas of some of the statues and paintings that grace the temple. They also provide background information on the Church of Jesus Christ of Latter-day Saints. ■

Square. The Mormon pioneers hauled the 782-pound (355-kilogram) bell to Utah all the way from Nauvoo, Illinois. The famous Mormon Tabernacle, a striking oval building with a silver dome, is a Utah landmark. The tabernacle was built in the 1860s, at a time when nails were scarce. The immense, vaulted ceiling is supported by a network of beams, held together by tightly fitted wooden pegs. This building is home to the celebrated Mormon Tabernacle Choir, a 320-voice choral group noted for its live performances and nationwide radio broadcasts.

On the square opposite the tabernacle is the Salt Lake Temple. The temple is not used for Sunday services, but for weddings, baptisms, and other sacred ceremonies or ordinances. The temple is built of massive granite blocks quarried at Little Cottonwood Canyon, 23 miles (37 km) away. Many of these blocks were carried to the building site on ox-drawn wagons. The temple is crowned by six spires. Atop the middle spire rests a gilded statue of the angel Moroni. The Mormons believe that Moroni appeared to Joseph Smith and revealed the gold plates on which the Book of Mormon was inscribed.

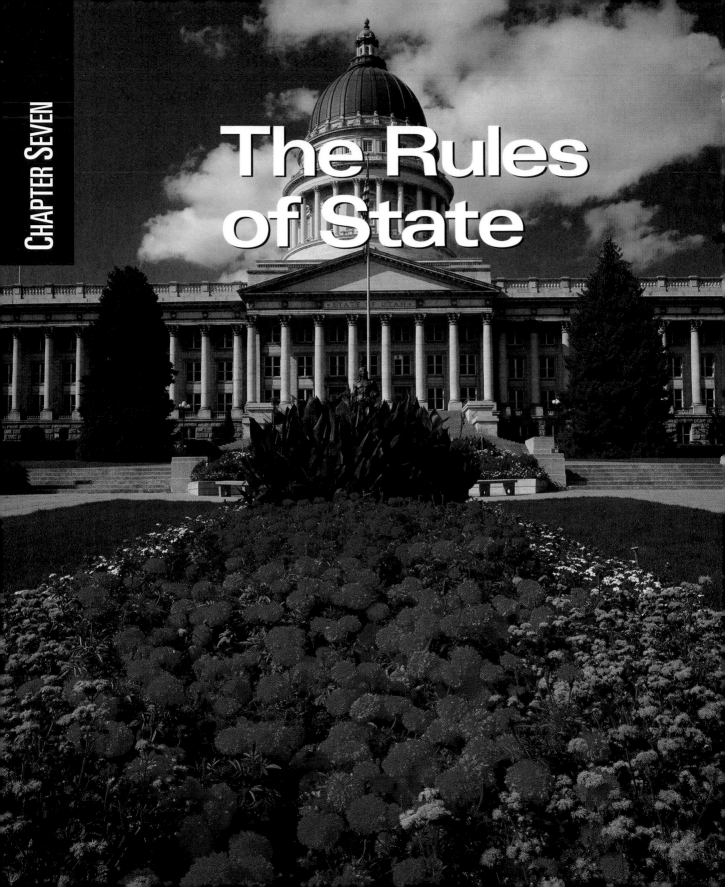

CHAPTER SEVEN

The Rules of State

Utah's state capitol stands on a hill overlooking Salt Lake City. Modeled on the U.S. Capitol in Washington, D.C., it is an imposing granite building with a great copper-plated dome. The capitol houses the legislature and the governor's office.

The capitol rotunda

The Balance of Power

Utah's constitution is the body of laws by which the state is governed. The constitution was adopted in 1895, a few months before Utah became a state. It divides the government into three main branches, like the branches of the federal government in Washington. The executive branch, or governor's office, makes sure that the laws are carried out. The legislative branch makes and repeals laws. The judicial branch, or court system, interprets the laws. In this way, the branches balance one another, and no single branch can become too powerful.

Utah's legislature has two divisions, or houses. The upper house, or senate, has twenty-nine members. There are seventy-five members in the lower house, or house of representatives. Senators are elected to four-year terms, while representatives serve two-year terms. No legislator may hold office for more than twelve consecutive years. The legislative session begins on the second Monday in January and normally lasts forty-five days. At any time, the governor may call for a special session of up to thirty days.

Opposite: The state capitol

The Scott Matheson Court Building, which houses Utah's supreme court

Utahns involved in minor disputes or accused of misdemeanors usually must appear before a local judge known as a justice of the peace. Depending on the community, justices of the peace are either appointed or elected. Felony cases and major civil suits are heard in Utah's seven district courts. District court judges are elected to six-year terms. Utah also has circuit courts and juvenile courts.

Cases from the lower courts can be appealed to Utah's supreme court, located in the Scott Matheson Court Building. The supreme court has five judges, or justices, who are elected to ten-year terms. The judge who has served the longest on the supreme court acts as its chief justice. In 1984 Utah's legislature approved the creation of an intermediate court to reduce the supreme court's caseload.

The governor of Utah may be elected to serve three consecutive

Utah's Governors

Name	Party	Term	Name	Party	Term
Heber M. Wells	Rep.	1896–1905	Herbert B. Maw	Dem.	1941–1949
John C. Cutler	Rep.	1905–1909	J. Bracken Lee	Rep.	1949–1957
William Spry	Rep.	1909–1917	George D. Clyde	Rep.	1957–1965
Simon Bamberger	Dem.	1917–1921	Calvin L. Rampton	Dem.	1965–1977
Charles R. Mabey	Rep.	1921–1925	Scott M. Matheson	Dem.	1977–1985
George H. Dern	Dem.	1925–1933	Norman H. Bangerter	Rep.	1985–1993
Henry H. Blood	Dem.	1933–1941	Michael O. Leavitt	Rep.	1993–

four-year terms. He or she must approve all laws, or bills, that are passed by the legislature. If the governor vetoes, or rejects, a bill, the legislature may still be able to override the governor's veto with a two-thirds vote in each house.

On the local level, Utah is divided into twenty-nine counties. Each county is governed by a three-member board of commissioners. Cities and towns operate under either a mayor and council or a council-manager form of government.

Governor Michael O. Leavitt

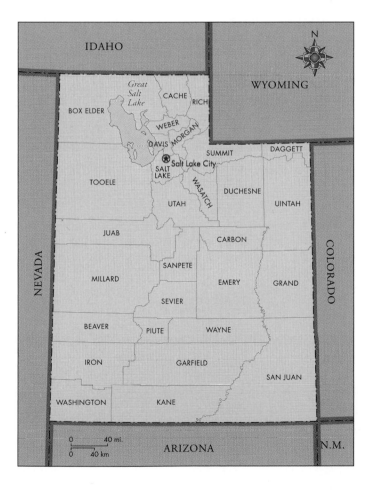

Utah's counties

Utah's State Flag and State Seal

Utah's state flag was adopted in 1913 and has a blue field fringed with gold. In the center is a gold circle containing the state coat of arms and the date 1896, the year Utah became a state.

The state seal has a beehive on a shield between two U.S. flags. A bald eagle perches on top of the shield. Above the shield are six arrows, and beneath is the date 1847, the year the first Mormon pioneers reached Utah. The coat of arms is edged with sego lilies, the state flower. ∎

Utah's State Song
"Utah, We Love Thee"

The words and music to Utah's state song were written by Evan Stephens. The song was officially adopted by Utah in 1917.

Land of the mountains high,
Utah, we love thee,
Land of the sunny sky, Utah, we
love thee!
Far in the glorious west, throned
on the mountain's crest,
In robes of statehood dressed,
Utah, we love thee!

Columbia's brightest star, Utah,
we love thee,
Thy luster shines afar, Utah, we
love thee!
Bright in our banner's blue,
among her sisters true
She proudly comes to view,
Utah, we love thee!

Land of the pioneers, Utah, we
love thee,
Grow with the coming years,
Utah, we love thee!
With wealth and peace in store,
to fame and glory soar,
God guarded, evermore, Utah,
we love thee!

Utah's State Symbols

State flower: Sego lily The bulbs of Utah's state flower (right) are edible. During the first hard years of settlement, the sego lily saved many of the pioneers from starvation.

State bird: Seagull Large numbers of seagulls can be found at Great Salt Lake and Utah Lake. According to legend, during the summer of 1848, hordes of crickets threatened to devour the settlers' crops. A flock of gulls appeared just in time, gobbling up the crickets and saving the food supply. Naturally, the seagull was selected as Utah's state bird.

State tree: Blue spruce This sturdy evergreen is common in the forests on Utah's mountains.

State mammal: Rocky mountain elk The elk is prized by hunters for its elegant rack of antlers. At preserves such as Hardware Ranch east of Hyrum, elk are protected and fed during the winter to keep them from foraging on nearby farms.

State fish: Rainbow trout This sleek, graceful fish is a native of Utah's rivers and freshwater lakes and a popular catch with fishers. It is a fierce fighter when caught.

State insect: Honeybee The state insect is a symbol of industry and community, two concepts that Utahns value deeply.

State gem: Topaz The topaz is a semiprecious stone that may be yellow, blue, or brown. In its purest form, it is almost colorless and can be found in the Thomas Range in western Utah. When heated, the stone turns pink. This "burnt topaz" is often used in jewelry.

State mineral: Copper Mined in many areas throughout the state, copper is an important commodity in Utah's economy.

State rock: Coal This important rock is found in seventeen of the twenty-nine counties in Utah. It originates as plant matter that develops in wetlands and bogs and is then covered by sediment over time. Coal is mined mostly in Emery County and Carbon County.

State fossil: Allosaurus Found more often around the state than any other dinosaur fossil, allosaurus fossils are the remnants of dinosaurs that once roamed what is now Utah.

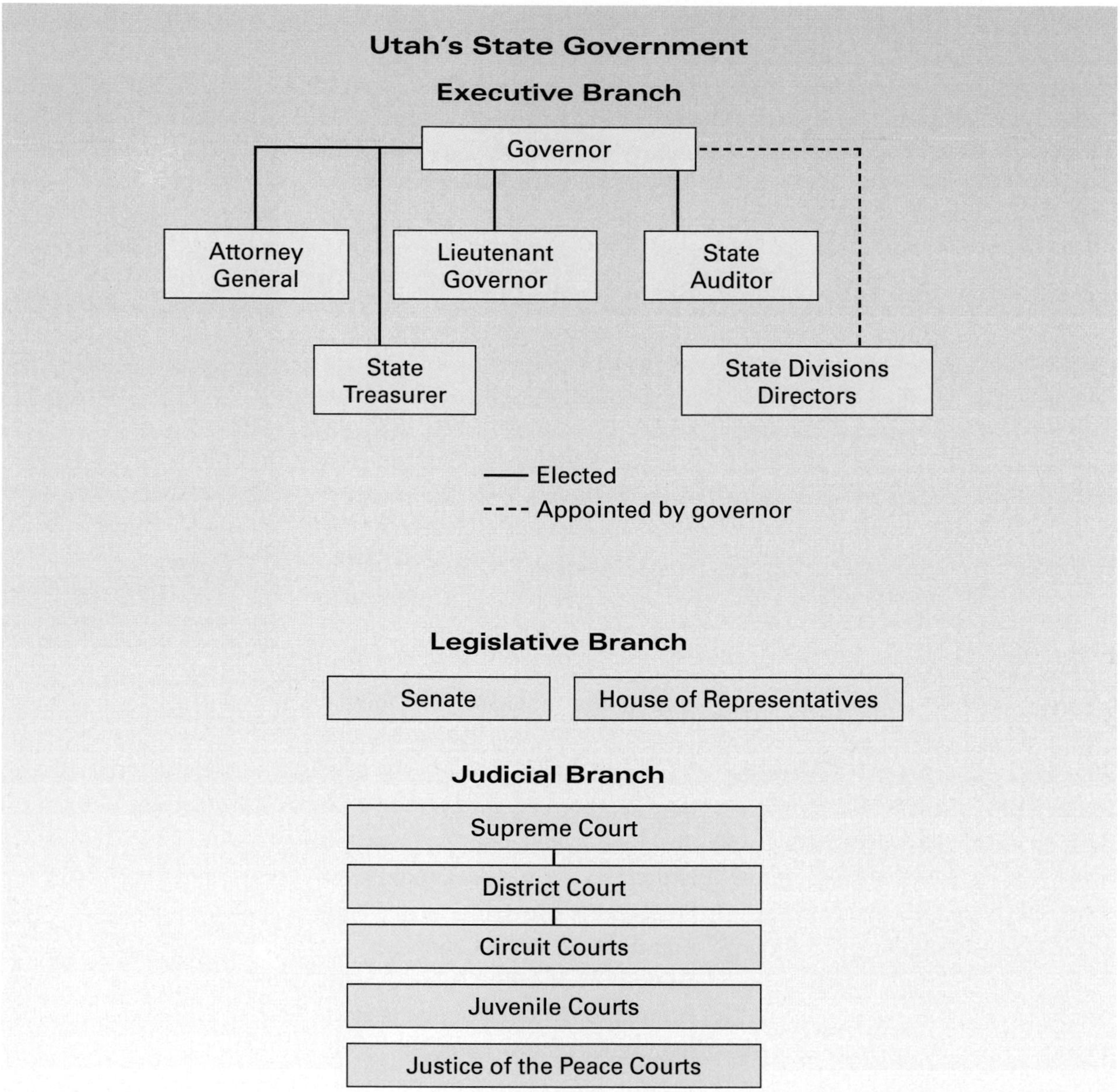

Utah's State Government

Executive Branch

Governor

Attorney General

Lieutenant Governor

State Auditor

State Treasurer

State Divisions Directors

—— Elected

---- Appointed by governor

Legislative Branch

Senate

House of Representatives

Judicial Branch

Supreme Court

District Court

Circuit Courts

Juvenile Courts

Justice of the Peace Courts

The Senator in the Capsule

Edwin Jacob (Jake) Garn (1932–) was born in Richfield. He ran an insurance company until 1972, when he was elected mayor of Salt Lake City. In 1974, Utahns elected Garn to represent them in the U.S. Senate. He served for eighteen years, retiring in 1992. During his long Senate career, Garn held prominent positions on several committees, including the Senate Appropriations Committee and the Committee on Housing and Urban Affairs. Garn earned national recognition in 1985 when he took a ride in the *Discovery* space shuttle. He circled the globe 109 times before splashdown. ■

Politics as Usual

Utahns tend to be politically conservative. They favor low taxes (although they have the highest taxes in the West) and wide opportunities for business. With the exceptions of Franklin Roosevelt and Harry Truman, Utahns have voted for Republican presidential candidates throughout the twentieth century. As is evident by the strong Republican showing on the national scene, Utahns heavily favor Republican candidates in their state and local governments.

The Rebel Republican

Elected to the U.S. Senate on the Republican ticket in 1977, Utah's Orrin Hatch (1934–) was a loyal supporter of Republican president Ronald Reagan during the 1980s. Yet Hatch is sometimes considered a rebel by his own party. He strongly supports business and religious interests that are dear to most Republicans. But he also pushes many Democratic agendas, such as health-care reform and compensation for people exposed to radiation from nuclear testing. Politics is not Hatch's only interest. He is a devout Mormon and composes religious songs in his spare time. ■

CHAPTER EIGHT

The Hive of Industry

A central emblem on Utah's state seal is a beehive. The honey-bee has been designated Utah's state insect. The bee, tire-lessly gathering nectar and turning it into stores of honey, demon-strates the virtues of hard work. Utahns have been extremely hard workers ever since the first settlers arrived in 1847. It is little won-der that they chose one word as their state motto: "Industry."

Utah farms prosper in spite of the dry climate.

To Market, to Market!

According to a 1996 study, the average American spends thirty-nine hours per week at work. Utahns, however, put in an average of forty-eight hours per week on the job. Not surprising, Utah has one of the fastest-growing state economies in the United States. Utah has long been a high producer of minerals and farm products. In recent years, the state has also vaulted into the field of high-tech manufacturing. Mining, agriculture, and manufacturing account for 20 percent of Utah's gross state product, or GSP—the total value of goods and services produced in the state.

Opposite: Harvesting apples

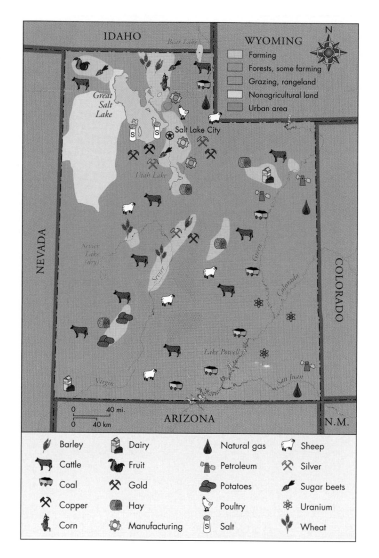

Map legend (top right of map):

IDAHO   WYOMING   N

- Farming
- Forests, some farming
- Grazing, rangeland
- Nonagricultural land
- Urban area

Great Salt Lake
Bear Lake
Salt Lake City
Utah Lake
Sevier Lake (dry)
Sevier
Green
Colorado
Lake Powell
San Juan
Virgin

NEVADA

COLORADO

0   40 mi.
0   40 km

ARIZONA   N.M.

Map key:

Barley		Dairy		Natural gas		Sheep	
Cattle		Fruit		Petroleum		Silver	
Coal		Gold		Potatoes		Sugar beets	
Copper		Hay		Poultry		Uranium	
Corn		Manufacturing		Salt		Wheat	

Utah's natural resources

Visitors to Utah are often amazed by its prosperous farms, a stunning patchwork of green fields amid the state's naturally parched valleys and hillsides. Utahns have created an elaborate system of reservoirs to water their crops. About 13,000 working farms cover some 20 percent of the state's land. About 25 percent of Utah's farmland is devoted to crops, such as hay, wheat, corn, barley, and potatoes. The state also has orchards of apples, peaches, and pears.

Most cattle growers in south-central Utah produce beef. Some beef cattle also graze in the region east of Salt Lake City, but this is chiefly dairy country. Utah is an important sheep-raising state. It also produces hogs, chickens, and turkeys.

Petroleum is Utah's most valuable mineral resource. Oil rigs sprout in Duchesne, San Juan, and Uintah Counties. Carbon, Sevier, and Emery Counties are the state's leading coal producers. Utah's coal is in increased demand because of its low sulfur content. When burned, low-sulfur coal causes relatively little air pollution in contrast with the high-sulfur variety. Natural gas is found in southeastern Utah.

Grilled Rainbow Trout

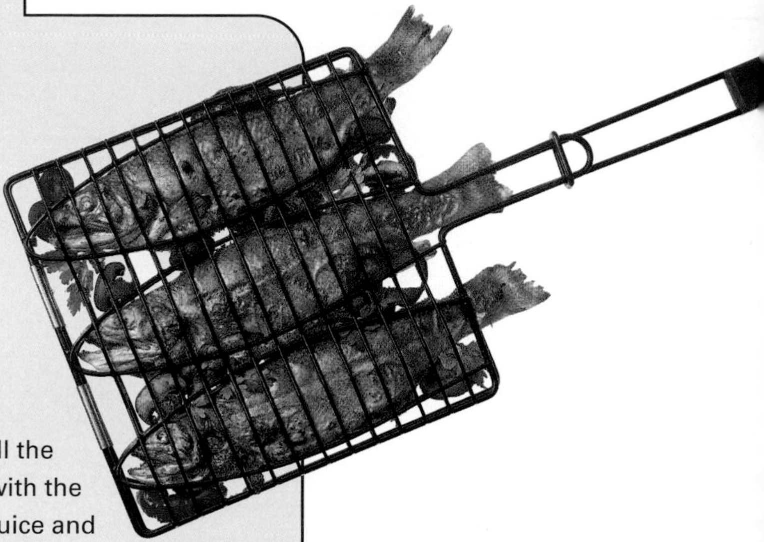

Rainbow trout is Utah's state fish.

Ingredients:

- 4 whole trout, cleaned
- 1 onion, chopped
- 3 tomatoes, seeded and chopped
- 1 lemon
- salt and pepper

Directions:

Ask an adult to prepare an outdoor grill. Fill the inside cavities of the cleaned whole trout with the onion and tomato. Squeeze a little lemon juice and sprinkle salt and pepper to taste inside each trout. Wrap the trout in tinfoil and place on the grill, cooking each side for approximately 10 minutes. Before serving the fish, unwrap them and check to make sure that the flesh is tender and cooked all the way through.

You can also cook the trout under the broiler. Fill each fish's cavity with the onion, tomato, lemon juice, and seasonings, then brush the outside of the fish with oil. Place on a rack and broil for approximately five minutes on each side, until the fish are done.

For a different flavor, you can substitute a sprig of fresh rosemary for the onion, tomato, and seasonings.
Serves 4.

Utah produces many valuable mineral ores. A few gold mines are active in Tooele County. Mines in Iron County harvest veins of silver. Magnesium and salt are taken from Great Salt Lake. Uranium deposits are found in the southeast around Moab. Utah is the second-biggest producer of copper in the United States. The Bing-

Copper mining is an important industry in Utah.

ham Copper Mine, operated by the Kennecott Copper Company, is the biggest open-pit copper mine in the world. Its yawning crater, in the Oquirrh Mountains west of Salt Lake City, is 2.5 miles (4 km) across.

Manufacturing accounts for 15 percent of Utah's GSP. The state's foremost manufactured product is transportation equipment. Factories in Brigham City make solid-fuel rocket propulsion systems for spacecraft and weapons. Utah's second most important manufactured product is primary metals, including steel and aluminum. Utah factories also turn out processed foods such as cheeses and packaged baked goods. Workers in the state assemble many types of scientific instruments, such as navigation systems for ships and planes.

What Utah Grows, Manufactures, and Mines

Agriculture	Manufacturing	Mining
Beef cattle	Food products	Coal
Milk	Primary metals	Copper
	Printed materials	Natural gas
	Scientific instruments	Petroleum
	Transportation equipment	

A-Plus!

One day in 1983, a group of students from Brigham Young University visited the chief executive officer (CEO) of Novell, a newly established computer manufacturer in Provo. For a class project, the students had designed a program that would enable personal computers to communicate with one another. The CEO was impressed. He believed that the new program would be valuable in offices where many people worked at small computers. He shifted Novell's focus from hardware to software and began to market NetWare, the program the students had devised.

Novell occupies a sprawling complex (above) of ten buildings at the south end of Provo. About 3,000 people work at the company's Provo headquarters, with another 600 at a branch office in San Jose, California. Novell is now designing a variety of programs that enhance access to the Internet. But NetWare is still one of its leading products. ■

Serving the Public

Service industries comprise 75 percent of Utah's GSP. People who work in service industries do not produce goods for sale. Instead they perform services for individuals or groups of people. Beauticians, sales clerks, teachers, lawyers, and physicians are all involved in service industries.

In Utah, the biggest portion of the service sector is community service and business. Many small businesses took root in Utah during the 1980s and 1990s. A large number of these businesses are devoted to information technology. Nearly 40,000 Utahns work in this rapidly growing field. For many years, the popular computer program WordPerfect, in its many versions, was produced in the Utah town of Orem. In the mid 1990s, WordPerfect moved from Utah to Canada.

Salt Lake City is Utah's financial center. It serves as headquarters for several credit-card companies. First Security is the largest bank in the state. Many Utahns work in government service.

The Man Who Loved Games

"I like the fact that game design is still a career option for young adults today," said Nolan Kay Bushnell (1943–) in an interview. Bushnell, who grew up in Ogden, Utah, spoke from experience. Games have been his pleasure and life's work, and they made him a fortune. In 1972, he invented Pong, the world's first video game. He went on to found Atari, which became one of the top producers of electronic games in the world. Eventually Bushnell sold Atari to Warner Brothers and retired from business. But his fascination with electronic possibilities has never died. Enthusiastically, he once proclaimed, "The Web is the world!" ■

Heroic Measures

In 1982, a Utah dentist named Barney Clark became an international celebrity. Clark, who was dying of heart disease, used the world's first artificial heart at the University of Utah Medical Center in Salt Lake City. The artificial heart was a giant machine stationed beside Clark's bed. Twenty-four hours a day it pumped without ceasing, circulating Clark's blood throughout his body. Barney Clark survived on the artificial heart for sixteen weeks, making medical history. Unfortunately, however, the machine has not yet been developed for widespread use. ■

Government jobs include teaching in the public schools, working in state or national parks, and membership in the military.

Making Connections

During its early years of white settlement, Utah was severely isolated from the rest of the world. That isolation was broken when telegraph wires spanned the territory in 1861. The transcontinental railroad, completed in 1869, proved to be a still more important link to the world outside. Ten railroad lines crisscross the state, mainly providing freight service. Utah has 43,000 miles (69,187 km) of paved roads, including 940 miles (1,512 km) of interstate highways, and is rebuilding a large portion of its freeways. A light-rail line, also in the works, will connect downtown Salt Lake City with the suburbs to the south. Salt Lake City has Utah's only international airport. The state also has eighty-seven smaller airfields.

The *Deseret News*, Utah's first newspaper, was founded in Salt

Remembering the Golden Spike

On May 10, 1869, a cheering crowd gathered at a lonely spot called Promontory Point, Utah, to witness a historic ceremony. Leland Stanford, chief partner of the Central Pacific Railroad Company, wielded a mighty hammer to drive in a golden spike. The ceremony marked the completion of North America's first transcontinental railroad. For four years, the Central Pacific had pushed eastward from San Francisco, while another company, the Union Pacific, laid track westward from St. Joseph, Missouri. Now at last the two tracks would be joined.

Ironically, Stanford's hammer missed the golden spike with its first blow. But a faithful telegraph operator ignored the embarrassing mishap and sent the message that all had gone well: "The last rail is laid, the last spike is driven. The Pacific Road is finished."

Every year on May 10, Utahns and visitors gather at the Golden Spike National Historic Site at Promontory. They come to reenact the 1869 ceremony, golden spike and all. Replicas (pictured above) of two 1869 locomotives touch noses on the completed tracks. ■

Bringing in the Picture

In 1921, everyone was excited about radio, the newest modern phenomenon. But a fifteen-year-old boy from Beaver, Utah, realized that radio was only the beginning. There had to be a way to add pictures to the sound. Philo Taylor Farnsworth (1906–1971) de-signed a television set for a high-school science project. His fascination with television continued, and he publicly demonstrated his first working television set in 1934. By the time he died, he had patented 160 different components for televisions and radios. ∎

Lake City in 1850. The Mormon-sponsored *Deseret News* also remains very popular. Utah has about fifty-five newspapers. The *Salt Lake City Tribune* has the largest circulation. Other papers in the state include the *Ogden Standard-Examiner* and the *Provo Daily Herald*. Utah has ninety-three radio stations and twenty television and cable stations. Four cable-TV systems operate within the state.

CHAPTER NINE

Getting to Know the Utahns

Every year on July 24, towns all over Utah celebrate Pioneer Day. With fireworks, speeches, and parades, Utahns honor the Mormon settlers who arrived in the Salt Lake Valley, led by Brigham Young. Mormonism has had a powerful influence on Utah since 1847, but people of many other backgrounds also make their homes in the state. They, too, have made their mark.

The people of Utah enjoy celebrating their history.

The Wasatch Front and Beyond

According to 1997 population estimates, Utah has 2,059,148 people. On average, Utah has 20 persons per square mile (8 per sq km), compared with the national average of 69 persons per square mile (27 per sq km). This figure creates the misleading impression that most Utahns live in wide-open spaces. The reality is quite different. Utah's population is clustered along the Wasatch Front, the western side of the Wasatch Range in the north-central part of the

Opposite: Biking in Moab

Population of Utah's Major Cities (1990)

Salt Lake City	159,963
West Valley City	86,976
Provo	86,835
Sandy	75,058
Orem	67,561
Ogden	63,909

state. The rest of Utah—the Great Basin, the Uinta Mountains, the canyonlands—is almost empty. Because of this population distribution, 87 percent of all Utahns are classified as urban dwellers— that is, they live in towns of 2,500 people or more. Only 13 percent of Utah's population is classified as rural.

Though Utah is primarily an urban state, most of its cities are relatively small. Salt Lake City, the capital, is the only city with more than 100,000 people. With its surrounding suburbs, Salt

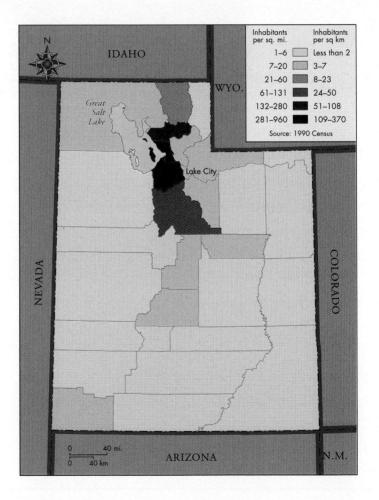

Inhabitants per sq. mi.		Inhabitants per sq km
1–6		Less than 2
7–20		3–7
21–60		8–23
61–131		24–50
132–280		51–108
281–960		109–370

Source: 1990 Census

Utah's population density map

Lake City is the biggest metropolitan area in the state. Following Salt Lake City in size are West Valley City, Provo, Sandy, Orem, and Ogden. Utah is one of the fastest-growing states in the nation. Because of its high birth rate and an influx of newcomers from outside the state, Utah's population jumped almost 20 percent between 1990 and 1997.

About 94 percent of all Utahns are of European ancestry. The majority of these people have an English, German, or Scandinavian background. Some 85,000 people with Spanish surnames live in the state, most of them with roots in Mexico. Asians and Pacific Islanders comprise the largest nonwhite segment of the population, numbering about 33,000. About 12,000 Utahns are African-American.

Utah's 24,000 Native Americans represent the Ute, Shoshone, Goshute, and Paiute. More than 2 million acres (810,000 ha) of

Asians are among the ethnic groups who live in Utah today.

Ringing in the New

Utahns ring in the new year with a gala festival in Temple Square. From all over the state, people gather to celebrate together. With music, food, and crafts, the festival embodies every aspect of Utah's cultural blend. Booths sell Navajo fry bread, Shoshone beadwork, and Mexican tacos. The notes of a bagpipe band interweave with the lively strains of salsa music. At the stroke of midnight, the square erupts in wild cheers and applause. ■

Utah's land is devoted to Indian reservations. The combined Uintah and Ouray Reservations in northeastern Utah are the largest in the state. The smaller Skull Valley and Goshute Reservations lie in the Great Basin area. A small portion of the vast Navajo Reservation of Arizona and New Mexico penetrates the Four Corners region in the southeast.

Keeping the Faith

With its close ties to Mormonism, Utah is unique among all the states. The church controls many of Utah's businesses, including banks, insurance companies, real estate firms, and the Zion Cooperative Mercantile Institute (ZCMI), the biggest department store in Salt Lake City. Mormons are involved in education and politics and produce the *Deseret News*, one of the state's leading papers.

A Mormon Sunday service

Roots

To baptize the dead, the Mormons need to know their names and something of their history. For this reason, they keep detailed records on their ancestors and on the families of Gentiles as well. An ever-expanding library of these genealogical records is housed in a maze of tunnels at the mouth of Cottonwood Canyon near Salt Lake City.

The Mormon records (above) are also a treasure trove of information for scientists as they try to unravel the mysteries of human genetics. ■

The Book of Mormon is the centerpiece of the Mormon religion. The book tells the story of two of the Lost Tribes of Israel, the Nephites and the Lamanites, who made their way to the New World. The light-skinned Nephites prospered for a time, but eventually they grew proud and greedy. Finally they were defeated by

The Bishop from Ireland

Lawrence Scanlan (1843–1915) arrived in Salt Lake City from Ireland in 1873. Scanlan was appointed to serve as Utah's first bishop, building a religious community for the small but growing number of Roman Catholics in the territory. In 1890, he bought property not far from Temple Square, where he ordered the construction of the Cathedral of the Madeleine. Completed in 1926, the cathedral is a highly ornate building with beautiful stained-glass windows. It remains a city landmark today. ■

the dark-skinned Lamanites, whom the Mormons believe were the ancestors of Native Americans.

In some important ways, Mormonism differs from other Christian denominations. According to Mormon doctrine, human beings can be deified—that is, they can become gods by living a holy life. Mormons also believe that God and his angels still speak to human beings directly, as they did in Biblical times, and that the soul may live many lives. Through baptism, even the dead can receive salvation. Thus Mormons practice two forms of baptism. Children are baptized into the faith at about the age of eight. Baptism ceremonies are also held for the dead.

The Mormons do not hire special pastors to run their church services. Instead, members of the community serve as church leaders. Beginning at the age of twelve, boys are brought into church affairs. At nineteen, young men leave home to spend two years as missionaries. These men, called "elders" because of their position in the church, carry the message of Mormonism throughout the world.

About 70 percent of all Utahns are Mormons. But many other faiths also flourish in the state. The next-largest religious group in Utah is Roman Catholic, with some 66,000 members. About 3,000 Utahns are Jewish. Many Protestant churches stand in Utah cities. These include Baptist, Presbyterian, Methodist, and Episcopalian.

The Love of Learning

Utahns are deeply committed to education. Among all the states, Utah has one of the highest percentages of high school graduates, and few other states have such a high percentage of citizens with college diplomas.

In fall 1847, almost as soon as they arrived in the Salt Lake Valley, Utah's pioneers organized a school. A seventeen-year-old schoolmistress named Mary Dilworth taught thirty pupils in a tent. By 1854, Utah Territory had 200 official schoolhouses. To send their children to one of these early school programs, parents usually had to pay a monthly fee. In 1890, Utah passed a law to fund free public elementary schools. Public high schools were authorized under the constitution in 1895.

Worker Bees

For children in early Utah, the most important learning went on outside the schoolroom. Parents and grandparents taught their children the skills they needed. Boys learned to hunt, plant, and harvest, while girls were taught cooking and sewing. One visitor commented that the purpose of education in Utah was "to rear a swarm of healthy working bees. The social hive has as yet no room for drones, book-worms, and gentlemen." ∎

Do You Speak Swahili? Ibo? Tagalog?

In 1997, Mormon missionaries fanned out to 113 countries. Because they travel so widely, the Mormons have an intense interest in foreign languages. Brigham Young University offers one of the most extensive language programs in the world. In addition to Spanish, French, and German, students can study many of the languages spoken in Africa, Asia, and the Pacific Islands. ■

The University of Deseret opened in Salt Lake City in 1867. In 1892, the name was changed to the University of Utah. The school moved in 1900 to a site at the eastern edge of Salt Lake City, where it is located today. One of only two private four-year colleges

Utah State University in Logan

in Utah, Brigham Young University was founded at Provo in 1875 as an institution for training teachers. Brigham Young has an outstanding reputation in the field of high technology. Utah's second private four-year college is Westminster College in Salt Lake City. Other schools of higher learning include Southern Utah University in Cedar City, Utah State University in Logan, and Weber State University in Ogden.

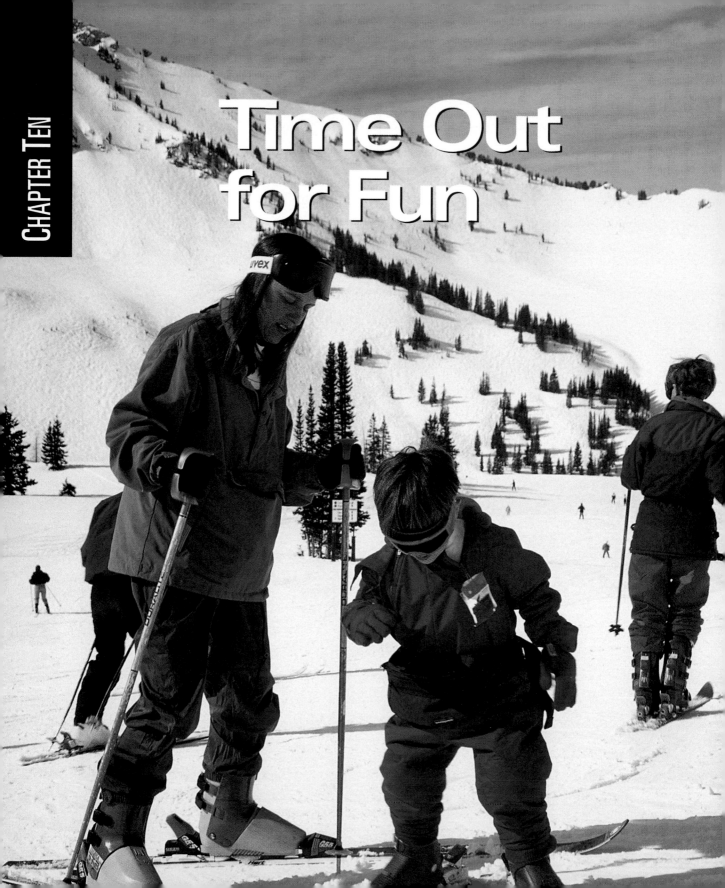

CHAPTER TEN

Time Out for Fun

M dway between Ogden and Salt Lake City, highway signs point to Lagoon Amusement Park. On summer days, the park is a glorious fun fest, bright with the gleeful shrieks of children as they zoom down the roller coaster. The park is a sprawling playground for people on the Wasatch Front. Sometimes it has as many as 15,000 visitors a day.

Outsiders often think that Utahns are somber folks who live to work, people who seldom enjoy life's lighter moments. Most Utahns are never afraid to have a good time, however. They love sports, music, art, and many other expressions of life's endless possibilities.

The historic wooden roller coaster at Lagoon Amusement Park thrills visitors.

Utah's "Zz" Teams

Utahns are passionate about basketball. The pride of the state is the Utah Jazz, which plays at the Delta Center in Salt Lake City. In

Opposite: Skiing at Alta

Utah Jazz forward Karl Malone (left) often relies on assists from guard John Stockton (right).

1979, the Jazz transferred from New Orleans, the jazz capital of the world, bringing its name to the Wasatch Front. Jazz forward Karl Malone is a Utah legend. Malone earned the nickname "the Mailman" because he is so adept at delivering the ball to the basket. He and his sidekick, point guard John "Stock" Stockton, are an invincible duo. The Jazz made the NBA Finals in 1997 and 1998, but were defeated for the championship by the Chicago Bulls.

Utah has no major-league football or baseball teams. But Utah citizens are proud of their Triple-A baseball team, the Buzz. Utahns

Utah's Playground

Lagoon Amusement Park is not only a place for wild rides. It is a site with a long history. The park opened in 1886 on the shores of Great Salt Lake and was originally known as Lakeside. Railroad tycoon Simon Bamberger created the park as a destination for train passengers, hoping to bring his company increased business. The park stands about 4 miles (6 km) east of its original location. It still has a wooden roller coaster from 1921 and a carousel that dates back to 1900. Lagoon Amusement Park is the second-oldest amusement park in operation in the United States. ■

Packing a Punch

Born in West Jordan, Utah, Gene Fullmer (1932–) held the National Boxing Association Middleweight Championship from 1959 until 1962. In the ring, Fullmer earned the nickname "Cyclone Gene" for his power and speed. After he retired, he returned to West Jordan, where his grandfather once farmed a homestead. "I had a terrific time taking some terrible beatings," Fullmer recalled in an interview. "Now I just raise a few pigs and a few horses, and I lose money on all of them." ■

also enjoy professional hockey. The Utah Grizzlies hockey team moved to Salt Lake City in 1995. Utah also hosts a professional women's basketball team, the Starzz. The state has other minor-league teams in hockey and baseball.

In college sports, Utahns cheer for the Running Utes, who play basketball at the University of Utah. The University of Utah's women's gymnastics team, the Red Rocks, won four NCAA championships in the 1990s.

The Cougars of Brigham Young were college football national champions in 1984. Many football greats, such as Steve Young and Jim McMahon, have come from Brigham Young. One of the biggest sports events of the year occurs when Brigham Young University meets its rival, the University of Utah, on the football field. Many fans decorate their homes with the flag of the school they root for.

In addition to spectator sports, Utahns enjoy being active in the great outdoors. Within 90 miles (145 km) of Salt Lake City are eleven ski resorts. Businesspeople can leave their downtown offices and swoop down a snow-covered mountain less than two hours

Park City is one of Utah's most popular resorts.

later. Among the most popular slopes are those at Alta and Park City. Brian Head is a major ski resort outside Bryce Canyon National Park.

A growing number of Utahns and visitors have come to enjoy the sport of mountain biking. Mountain bikes are sturdy vehicles

Going for the Gold

During the late 1990s, Utahns threw themselves into preparations for the 2002 Winter Olympics, to be hosted by Salt Lake City. New highways were constructed to handle the increased traffic, and a new stadium, the Delta Center, was built for the occasion. Construction of the Olympic Village got underway on the University of Utah campus. Though Salt Lake City would be the hub of activity, the Olympics would be spread over much of the state. Many other towns planned to host specific events. These included Kearns (speed skating), Ogden (curling), Park City (snowboarding and giant slalom), and Provo (women's hockey). Utah's business community hoped that the Winter Olympics would promote tourism and commercial development in the state. They saw the Olympics not as an end in itself, but as a beginning. As one business leader explained, "You don't build all this infrastructure for an event that's over in sixteen days, any more than you build a church just for Easter." ■

with reinforced frames for added strength. The tires are thick and covered with bumps for gripping rugged terrain. For this reason, mountain bikes are sometimes called "fat tires" or "knobby tires." Mountain bikers pump their way up awesomely steep inclines and blast downhill full tilt. The Fat Tire Mountain Biking Festival brings hundreds of devotees to Moab each October.

To W. D. Rishel, a bicycle racer from Salt Lake City, the Bonneville Salt Flats seemed an ideal spot for riding fast. Rishel started a trend when he raced his bike across the flats in 1896. The automobile quickly replaced the bicycle as drivers experimented with speed on the open, level ground. In 1970, a driver named Gary Gabelich achieved the dizzying speed of 622.4 mph (1,001.4 kph) in a car with a rocket-powered engine. Rocket-powered vehicles no longer compete on the speedway, and many participants do not consider them to be "true" racing cars. ∎

Mountain biking in Utah's great outdoors

Another sporting event unique to Utah is "going to the salt." Every summer, race-car drivers gather to compete for speed records at the Bonneville Salt Flats. Whether their cars are vintage autos from the 1930s or sleek new solar-powered models, all are designed to move fast. Level as a tabletop, the speedway is 9 miles (14 km) long and 80 feet (24 m) wide. It is a perfect place for racers to step on the gas, pushing to break records set in bygone years. Unfortunately, however, heavy usage is causing the salt flats to deteriorate, crumbling a bit more each season.

Let There Be Music!

When the first settlers crossed the plains and mountains with Brigham Young, they brought all the essentials for starting a new life. They carried seed corn and plowshares, axes and spades. And in several heavy wooden crates they hauled the disassembled sections of a large pipe organ. To the Mormons, music was a necessity of life. Weeks after they reached the Salt Lake Valley, the settlers formed a choir to sing sacred songs. That singing group, founded in 1847, is the celebrated Mormon Tabernacle Choir. Its music is heard and loved throughout the world.

Until 1979, the Mormon Tabernacle was home to the Utah Symphony Orchestra. The orchestra now performs at Abravanel Hall, a block from Temple Square. The hall was named for Maurice Abravanel, who took charge of the symphony in 1947, seven years after its founding. Under his direction, the symphony won international acclaim. Since 1978, Salt Lake City residents have been dedicated supporters of the Utah Opera Company, which performs

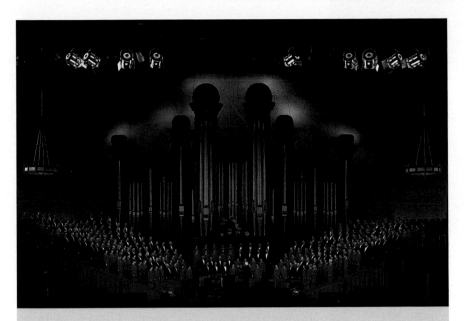

Make a Joyful Noise

On Thursdays and Sundays, visitors are welcome to attend rehearsals of the Mormon Tabernacle Choir in Salt Lake City. The choir consists of 320 women and men between the ages of thirty and sixty. Members may stay with the group for up to twenty years. Through its weekly broadcasts on NBC Radio, the choir reaches millions of people around the world. In its performances, the choir is accompanied by the enormous pipe organ in the Mormon Tabernacle. Some music lovers claim this organ has a special "signature tone" that they can recognize in any recording. ■

at Capitol Theatre. For those who like to know what the dramatics are all about, the theater flashes English supertitles on an overhead projector.

Utah has several noted dance companies. Ballet West is based at the University of Utah in Salt Lake City and also performs at the

Dancers from Ballet West

Capitol Theater. The Repertory Dance Theater, also based in Salt Lake City, began in 1966 with a grant from the Rockefeller Foundation. The small Ririe-Woodbury Dance Company performs innovative modern pieces.

Utahns enjoy theater, both musicals and dramatic productions. Brigham Young established the Deseret Musical and Dramatic Society in 1849. During the 1850s, a group of workers began to give performances, calling themselves the Mechanics Dramatic Association. The Pioneer Theatre puts on seven plays a year. Renowned stars from television and Broadway have performed on this stage. The Pioneer Theatre has a special interest in producing plays related to Utah history.

Utah has also found a major role in the highly competitive world of film. In 1980, Hollywood actor Robert Redford began the Sundance Film Institute in Park City. The institute is a forum for

Box Office Take

Cash was scarce in frontier Utah so the Mechanics Dramatic Association did not demand money in exchange for tickets. To see the show, theatergoers brought goods to barter. On one evening, the box office collected twenty bushels of wheat, five of corn, four of potatoes, and two of oats; plus four bushels of salt, a keg of applesauce, two hams, a live pig, a dog, a wolf skin, a set of embroidered children's underwear, and a silver coffin plate from Germany. ■

Robert Redford at his Sundance Film Festival

screenwriters and filmmakers who want to break away from the demands of the mass market. The Sundance Film Festival has been held in Park City each January since 1988. Thousands of critics, actors, producers, and film devotees flock to the festival each year to preview new movies that may or may not make it big. The Sundance Festival has grown so immensely popular that some have complained it has become thoroughly "mainstream."

Artists and Writers

Utahns have a deep appreciation of literature and art. The Utah Arts Council sends artists to schools in rural areas, where they hold workshops and demonstrations for the students. It promotes the revival of folk arts such as quilting and wood carving, which were in danger of dying out. The council also sponsors an annual statewide art competition. The Salt Lake City Arts Festival offers local artists the chance to show their work to the public.

Utah has many fine museums where outstanding works of art are displayed. The Brigham Young University Museum of Fine Arts and the Springville Museum of Art exhibit work by Utah artists. The two-level Salt Lake Arts Center in Salt Lake City hosts traveling exhibits from around the United States. It also honors the work of local painters and sculptors. A diverse collection of works

Legend of the Escalante

"I have always been unsatisfied with life as most people live it," wrote painter Everett Reuss (1914–1934?) shortly before he disappeared. "Always I want to live more intensely and richly. Why muck and conceal one's true longings and loves, when by speaking one might find someone to understand them, and by acting upon them one might discover one's true self?"

An artist of great promise, Reuss fell in love with the majestic scenery of Utah's canyon country. In the fall of 1934, he set out with two burros to spend the winter in the Grand Staircase region. He was never seen again, though search parties found his burros wandering the canyons in the spring. Most people believe that Reuss died in a fall or perished of exposure in a sudden storm.

Though he was only twenty when he died, Reuss survives as a Utah legend. Countless young artists are inspired by his love of beauty and wilderness, and by his determination to be true to himself. Reuss has been the subject of several biographies and even a motion picture. ■

from around the world is housed at the Utah Museum of Fine Arts, also in Salt Lake City.

One of the most famous writers to spend time in Utah was Mark Twain (1835–1910), who visited Salt Lake City in the late 1850s. Twain gave his impressions in his 1872 memoir of the Old West titled *Roughing It*. The popular writer of Western novels, Zane Grey, used the canyon country around the Green River as the setting of his tale *Robber's Roost*. Two authors have won the Pulitzer Prize for books about Utah's first white settlers. Bernard de Voto won the Pulitzer Prize for history in 1947 with his account of the

The Salt Lake City Arts Festival always draws a crowd.

Mormon pioneers titled *Across the Wide Missouri*. Wallace Stegner wrote *The Gathering of Zion* in 1964 and won the prize for fiction in 1972 with his novel *Angle of Repose*.

Utah's artists and writers give expression to their state's rich history and stunning natural beauty. For those who live there, and for the millions who visit each year, Utah holds boundless treasures that wait to be discovered.

Opposite: Utah's natural beauty has inspired artists and writers for generations.

Timeline

United States History

The first permanent English settlement is established in North America at Jamestown. **1607**

Pilgrims found Plymouth Colony, the second permanent English settlement. **1620**

America declares its independence from Britain. **1776**

The Treaty of Paris officially ends the Revolutionary War in America. **1783**

The U.S. Constitution is written. **1787**

The Louisiana Purchase almost doubles the size of the United States. **1803**

The United States and Britain **1812–15** fight the War of 1812.

Utah State History

c. 1350 The Anasazi cliff dwellers abandon their villages, migrating south and west.

1776 A small Spanish party, led by Father Silvestre Velez de Escalante and Father Francisco Atanasio Dominguez, sets out from Santa Fe, New Mexico, to find a route to California. They explore the area that is now Utah and return.

1811 A trapping expedition, sent by John Jacob Astor, reaches the mountains of western Utah.

1821 Spanish Utah becomes part of the Republic of Mexico after Mexico separates from Spain.

1824 James Bridger arrives at the Great Salt Lake. He is considered to be the first European to see the lake.

1847 Brigham Young and his party reach the Salt Lake Valley on July 24.

1848 The United States gains control of what is now Utah as a result of the Mexican-American War.

1848 According to Mormon history, a flock of seagulls rescue Mormon settlers, eating crickets that threaten their crops.

United States History

Utah State History

1850 The U.S. federal government rejects the State of Deseret's application for statehood and renames the region Utah.

1857 Utah Mormans and Paiute Indians attack a wagon train crossing Utah in the Mountain Meadow Massacre during the Utah War.

The North and South fight **1861–65** each other in the American Civil War.

1864 Utah Territory is divided when Nevada becomes a state.

1890 Wilfred Woodruff, president of the Mormon Church, advises Mormons to give up polygamy.

1896 Utah becomes the forty-fifth state on January 4.

The United States is **1917–18** involved in World War I.

1913 The U.S. Bureau of Land Reclamation builds the Strawberry River Reservoir, delivering water to Utah's deserts and aiding in the growth of the state's cattle industry.

The stock market crashes, **1929** plunging the United States into the Great Depression.

1929 Utah's mining industry collapses after the stock-market crash.

The United States **1941–45** fights in World War II.

The United States becomes a **1945** charter member of the U.N.

The United States **1951–53** fights in the Korean War.

1952 Uranium is discovered near Moab, leading to mining of the mineral for nuclear weapons.

The U.S. Congress enacts a series of **1964** groundbreaking civil rights laws.

The United States **1964–73** engages in the Vietnam War.

The United States and other **1991** nations fight the brief Persian Gulf War against Iraq.

1991 The U.S. government reimburses "downwinders" in Utah and other states for exposure to radiation experiments during the late 1950s and early 1960s.

Fast Facts

Utah state capitol

Statehood date	January 4, 1896, the 45th state
Origin of state name	From the Navajo word meaning "upper" or "higher up" as applied to a tribe called the Ute.
State capital	Salt Lake City
State nickname	Beehive State
State motto	"Industry"
State bird	Seagull
State flower	Sego lily
State mammal	Rocky Mountain elk
State insect	Honeybee
State fossil	Allosaurus
State mineral	Copper
State rock	Coal
State fish	Rainbow trout
State gem	Topaz

Sego lily

Copper mine

Wasatch Mountain Range

State song	"Utah, We Love Thee"
State tree	Blue spruce
State fair	Early September at Salt Lake City
Total area; rank	84,905 sq. mi. (219,904 sq km); 13th
Land; rank	82,169 sq. mi. (212,818 sq km);12th
Water; rank	2,736 sq. mi. (7,086 sq km); 14th
Inland water; **rank**	2,736 sq. mi. (7,086 sq km); 7th
Geographic center	Sanpete, 3 miles (4.8 km) north of Manti
Latitude and longitude	Utah is located approximately between 37° N and 42° N and 109° 03′ W and 114° 03′ W
Highest point	Kings Peak, 13,528 feet (4,126 m)
Lowest point	Beaverdam Creek in Washington County, 2,000 feet (610 m)
Largest city	Salt Lake City
Number of counties	29
Population; rank	1,727,784 (1990 census); 35th
Density	20 persons per sq. mi. (8 per sq km)
Population distribution	87% urban, 13% rural

Ethnic distribution (does not equal 100%)

White	93.79%
Hispanic	4.91%
Other	2.19%
Asian and Pacific Islanders	1.94%
Native American	1.41%
African-American	0.67%

Record high temperature	116°F (47°C) at St. George on June 28, 1892
Record low temperature	–50°F (–46°C) at Woodruff on February 6, 1899, and in Utah County on January 5, 1913
Average July temperature	73°F (23°C)
Average January temperature	25°F (–4°C)
Average annual precipitation	12 inches (30 cm)

Natural Areas and Historic Sites

National Historic Sites
Golden Spike honors the site where the Central Pacific and Union Pacific Railroads met during the construction of the transcontinental railroad in the nineteenth century.

National Parks
Arches has one of the largest concentrations of natural sandstone formations—such as arches and balancing rocks—in the world.

Bryce Canyon is renowned for its colorful sandstone, mudstone, and Claron limestone spires—called "hoodoos"—created from millions of years of erosion.

At *Canyonlands*, visitors can marvel at the breathtaking views from the Island in the Sky, or boat down the area called the Rivers.

Capitol Reef was created to preserve the Waterpocket Fold, a monocline—or groove in the earth's crust—that is 100 miles (161 km) long.

Zion sports Kolob Arch—the world's largest geological arch—which reaches a height of 310 feet (94.6 m).

Mesa arches

Cedars State Historical Monument

National Monuments

Cedar Breaks, near Cedar City, has been formed from erosion of the Pink Cliffs. The canyon's ridge, 10,000 feet (3,050 m) above sea level, is laced with forests and flowered meadows.

Dinosaur, where the Yampa River joins the Green River, is home to many endangered species, such as the peregrine falcon and bald eagle.

Hovenweep allows Native American enthusiasts to see cliff dwellings dating back to 500 B.C., built by early inhabitants of the Southwest's Four Corners area.

Natural Bridges is aptly named for the streams that have cut through sandstone over millions of years, creating bridges of natural stone.

Rainbow Bridge is the world's largest natural bridge. It is visited by 300,000 visitors each year and is sacred to Native Americans.

Timpanogos Cave, in the side of Mount Timpanogos, provides an interesting view of helictites, formations that point in all directions.

Grand Staircase-Escalante contains a remarkable rock formation whose "steps" are 900 feet (275 m) high.

National Recreation Areas

Glen Canyon, stretching from Lees Ferry in Arizona to the Orange Cliffs in Utah, gives tourists a chance to enjoy hiking and spectacular views.

National Forests

Utah has six national forests, among which are Uinta National Forest and Manti-LaSal National Forest. Visitors can marvel at the greenery and scenes of Utah's vast landscape.

State Parks

Utah has forty-five state parks: heritage, scenic, and recreational. Classified as heritage, This Is the Place State Park has a living historic village at Old Deseret. Goblin Valley State Park, in the scenic category, contains eroded bulbous rock formations. Piute State Park is recreational and offers year-round fishing as well as camping.

Grand Staircase-Escalante National Monument

John Stockton

Sports Teams

NCAA Teams (Division 1)

Brigham Young University Cougars

Southern Utah University Thunderbirds

University of Utah Utes

Utah State University Aggies

Weber State University Wildcats

National Basketball Association

Utah Jazz

Women's National Basketball Association

Utah Starzz

National Hockey League

Utah Grizzlies

Cultural Institutions

Libraries

The *Salt Lake City Public Library* system, including a main library and five branches throughout the city, contains various resources for research and entertainment.

The *Utah History Information Center* is the public research center for the State Historical Society of Utah. Visitors can access information about the history of the state and view materials from its collections.

The *Utah State Archives* allows users to research the history of the state.

The *Utah Valley Family History Library*, part of Brigham Young University, aids people in tracing their genealogy, in particular those of the Mormon faith.

Museums

The Beehive House in Salt Lake City was Brigham Young's home. Visitors can see furniture from the pioneer days and learn about how the Young family lived.

Brigham Young University

The *CEU Dinosaur Museum* in Price contains a reconstructed woolly mammoth whose bones were found intact, a giant sloth, and a collection of dinosaur bones.

The *Utah Museum of Fine Arts*, at the University of Utah in Salt Lake City, has a 15,000-piece collection of artworks.

Performing Arts
Utah has two major opera companies, two major dance companies, and one symphony orchestra.

Universities and Colleges
In the mid-1990s, Utah had ten public and seven private institutions of higher learning.

Annual Events

Robert Redford at Sundance Film Festival

January–March
Sundance Film Festival in Park City (January)

April–June
Easter Jeep Safari in Moab (April)

St. George Arts Festival (April)

Friendship Cruise in Green River (May)

Reenactment of the Driving of the Golden Spike at Promontory (May 10)

Scottish Festival in Salt Lake City (June)

Strawberry Days Festival in Pleasant Grove (June)

Tooele Arts Festival (June)

Utah Arts Festival in Salt Lake City (June)

July–September
Western Stampede in West Jordan (early July)

Days of '47 in Salt Lake City (week of July 24)

Pioneer Days in Ogden (week of July 24)

Salt Lake City Arts Festival

Mormon Miracle Pageant in Manti (July)

Ute Stampede in Nephi (July)

Festival of the American West in Logan (July and August)

Shakespearean Festival in Cedar City (July and August)

Park City Arts Festival (August)

Oktoberfest at Snowbird Resort, outside Salt Lake City (August to October)

Utah State Fair in Salt Lake City (September)

October–December

Fat Tire Mountain Biking Festival in Moab (October)

America's Opening in Park City (November)

Festival of Lights Parades in Bullfrog and at Lake Powell (November and December)

Christmas at Temple Square in Salt Lake City (December)

The Nutcracker at Utah State University in Logan and Salt Lake City (December)

The Messiah in the Mormon Tabernacle in Salt Lake City (Sunday before Christmas)

Jim Bridger

Famous People

Maude Adams (1872–1953)	Actress
Hal Ashby (1936–1988)	Film director and producer
James (Jim) Bridger (1804–1881)	Explorer and trapper
John Moses Browning (1855–1926)	Inventor
Butch Cassidy (1887–1912)	Outlaw
Patrick Edward Connor (1820–1891)	Military officer and anti-Mormon leader
Bernard Augustine de Voto (1897–1955)	Author

Marriner Stoddard Eccles (1890–1977)	Banker
Philo Taylor Farnsworth (1906–1971)	Engineer and inventor
Harvey Fletcher (1884–1981)	Physicist
John Charles Frémont (1813–1890)	Explorer and surveyor
Orrin Grant Hatch (1934–)	U.S. senator
Esther R. Landa (1912–)	Civil rights and women's activist
Donny (1958–) and Marie (1959–) Osmond	Entertainers
Jedediah Strong Smith (1799–1831)	Explorer and trapper
Joseph Smith (1805–1844)	Founder of Church of Jesus Christ of Latter-day Saints
Wakara (1808?–1855)	Ute chief
Wilford Woodruff (1807–1898)	Mormon leader
Brigham Young (1801–1877)	Mormon leader and territorial governor
Mahonri Mackintosh Young (1877–1957)	Sculptor, painter and etcher
Steven Young (1961–)	Professional football player

Brigham Young

To Find Out More

History

- Fradin, Dennis Brindell. *Utah*. Chicago: Childrens Press, 1993.

- Hickox, Rebecca. *Salt Lake City*. Parsippany, N.J.: Dillon, 1990.

- Sirvaitis, Karen. *Utah*. Minneapolis, Minn.: Lerner Publications, 1991.

- Thompson, Kathleen. *Utah*. Austin, Tex.: Raintree/Steck Vaughn, 1996.

Fiction

- Fitzgerald, John D. *The Great Brain*. New York: Yearling, 1972.

- Litchman, Kristin Embry, and Warren Chang (illustrator). *All Is Well*. New York: Delacorte, 1998.

Biographies

- Dolan, Sean. *James Beckwourth*. Broomall, Penn.: Chelsea House, 1992.

- Sanford, William R. *John C. Fremont: Soldier and Pathfinder*. Springfield, N.J.: Enslow Publishers, 1996.

- Simon, Charnan. *Brigham Young: Mormon and Pioneer*. Danbury, Conn.: Children's Press, 1999.

- Wukovitz, John F. *Butch Cassidy*. Broomall, Penn.: Chelsea House, 1997.

Websites

- **The State of Utah Navigational Network**
  http://www.state.ut.us
  The official website for the state of Utah

- **UtahLINK!**
  http://www.uen.org/utahlink/
  Connects users to resources on public and higher education

- **The Utah Travel Council**
  http://www.utah.com
  To find out about tourist spots and recreation in Utah

Addresses

- **Office of the Governor**
  210 State Capitol
  Salt Lake City, UT 84114
  To contact Utah's chief executive officer

- **Utah Arts Council**
  617 East South Temple
  Salt Lake City, UT 84102-1177
  To find information on arts events throughout the state

- **Utah Sports Authority**
  2108 State Office Building
  Salt Lake City, UT 84114
  Provides information on sporting events

- **Utah State Parks and Recreation**
  1594 West North Temple
  Suite 116
  Salt Lake City, UT 84114-6001
  To find out about the many state parks and other natural sites

Index

Page numbers in *italics* indicate illustrations.

Meet the Author

Deborah Kent grew up in Little Falls, New Jersey, where she was the first totally blind student to attend the local public school. She received a bachelor's degree in English from Oberlin College in Ohio. She earned a master's degree from Smith College School for Social Work and spent four years working in community mental health at the University Settlement House in New York City.

In 1975, Deborah Kent left social work to pursue her dream of becoming a writer. She moved to San Miguel de Allende, Mexico, a town with a thriving colony of foreign writers and artists. In San Miguel, she wrote her first book, *Belonging,* a novel for young adults. Kent is the author of fifteen novels and many nonfiction books for children. She lives in Chicago with her husband, children's author R. Conrad Stein, and their daughter, Janna.

Deborah Kent loves to travel and meet new people of diverse backgrounds. She especially likes to experience the outdoors by hiking and birding. With its extraordinary natural wonders, Utah is one of her favorite states.

Photo Credits

Photographs ©:

AP/Wide World Photos: 98 (Bill Beattie), 114 left (Michael Conroy), 114 right, 132 (Bill Janscha), 53, 91 top, 99
Archives Office of Diocese of Salt Lake City: 108
Bob Clemenz Photography: 100 (Bob & Suzanne Clemenz)
Corbis-Bettmann: 48, 55 (UPI), 30, 33, 37, 41, 42, 43, 135 bottom
Courtesy Administrative Office of the Courts: 86
Courtesy of Lieutenant Governor's Office: 88
Courtesy Office of the Governor: 87
Dave G. Houser: 93 (Jan Butchofsky), 116 (Rankin Harvey), 65, 69
Dembinsky Photo Assoc.: 67 (Mike Barlow), 7 top right, 112 (Mark E. Gibson), 62, 130 (Adam Jones), 89, 128 bottom (Rod Planck)
Envision: 95 (Steven Needham)
First Image West: 19 (Richard Weston)
LDS Church Visual Resources Library: 107, 119, 44 top
LDS Historical Department Archives: 47
Liaison Agency, Inc.: 52 (Hulton Getty), 91 bottom (Brad Markel), 121, 133 bottom (Smart)
New England Stock Photo: 74 (Jean Higgins), 58 (Michael J. Howell), 9 (Andre Jenny), 96, 129 top (Margo Pinlerton)

North Wind Picture Archives: 15, 17 top, 20, 26, 34, 36, 40, 46, 59
Novell: 97
Robert Holmes Photography: 102 (Markham Johnson), 7 bottom, 17 bottom, 92 (Dewitt Jones)
Salt Lake Convention and Visitors Bureau: 103, 105, 123, 134
Steve Greenwood: cover
Stock Montage, Inc.: 25, 27, 31, 32, 35, 44 bottom, 135 top
Superstock, Inc.: 38 bottom, 72
Tom Dietrich: 2, 110
Tom Till: 6 top right, 6 top left, 6 top center, 8, 12, 29, 56, 61, 63, 66, 71, 76, 77, 78, 82, 84, 85, 124, 128 top, 129 bottom, 131 bottom
Tony Stone Images: 7 top left, 117 (Dugald Bremner), 83 (Philip H. Coblentz), 18 (David Muench), 7 top center, 81 (Chuck Pefley), back cover (Jake Rajs), 14, 131 top (Tom Till)
Unicorn Stock Photos: 73 (Jean Higgins), 106 (A Ramey/CPI)
Utah State Historical Society: 22 (75029), 24 (14610), 38 top (10106), 39 (27710), 49 (3689), 50 (17821), 51 (534)
Utah Travel Council: 79 (Frank Jensen), 80, 133 top (John Telford), 113, 120
VIREO/Academy of Natural Sciences of Philadelphia: 6 bottom, 70 (R. & N. Bowers)
Maps by XNR Productions, Inc.